BARN
SECRETS

PETER ZIMMER

Paperback: 978-1-964035-55-0
eBook: 978-1-964035-56-7
Library of Congress Control Number: 2024926802

This is a work of nonfiction.

SWEETSPIRE LITERATURE
—— MANAGEMENT ——

Have you ever been driving down the road and passed an old barn and thought:

"I wonder what I would find in there?"

Table of Contents

Preface

*E*very book should be informative and/or entertaining. My hopes are that this might bring a smile to your face, a tear to your eye or joy to your heart, and if I am lucky you might say, I didn't know that!

This is a work mostly of fiction, although I have used a lot of my life experiences in it, some names used are people that I have known at some point in my life. They each have brought me happiness, joy, comfort or sorrow and every one of them has been informative. If you see your name in here, please know that I was thinking about you; not in the storyline necessarily, but as some inspiration for my putting this down in writing. If you get to a point and wonder, was this meant to insult, harm and degrade me? Please, know that the answer to that will always be no. My memories with my friends, families and acquaintances are all very cherished. I had an entire series of books in my head about the bad things in my life that have happened, either through my own bad judgment or poor decisions, but I have long since buried those.

What you would expect to find in a barn is farm stuff. The nondescript pieces of life on a farm have all been well documented by those much more knowledgeable about such things than me. I wanted to find the things that you would NOT expect to find there. The things that make life, friends, and families, interesting.

Forward

*T*his trip was not really involved in Barn Stories, but may shine a light on part of the evolution of the project.

In my earlier days I founded a medical laser service company out of the Midwest. Even as a kid I always wanted to run a business and had a fondness for technology. I was more of a loner as a kid and remember a good friend of mine later in life who told me that "If you can count your friends, your true friends, on one hand when you die, you have lived a good life."

I did not set out to gather friends, but I can look back and say that I have met a lot of phenomenal people. Some have guided me and everyone in my life has invested their time and helped mold me to keep looking for answers to questions.

In my business life I have had many start ups, few that could be considered successful and a few that gave me plenty of experience and ideas. When I finally found one that was to be successful, I found myself first traveling all over the midwest, then all over the country until I was able to develop some companies that allowed me to travel all over the world. Many conventions taught me how to live out of a suitcase and overcome whatever obstacles and problems that presented themselves.

On one of my many trips to the capital of convention cities I was laid over in between medical convention shows in Las Vegas. Since the booth and equipment were already there and I had a few days before the start of the next show, I took the rental car and decided to do a little exploring of the desert southwest. Having spent enough time in Las Vegas casinos and seen as many floor shows as I wanted, I headed east through Nevada and across the Hoover Dam and out into the great expanse of Arizona which I knew nothing about.

Skip the interstates, I wanted to see the land that I was forever flying over to get to somewhere else. Looking out of an airplane window while cruising at thirty thousand feet and seeing the roads and towns with a cocktail while fixating on one set of lights of a car, truck, or semi, invited me to wonder: where was THIS one set of lights heading? What story might one of them have that no one knows about? A delivery? A run to a loved one? Maybe to a hospital for that last goodbye….

This trip into Arizona took me down a very poor looking stretch of road interrupted by lots of rocks and more than a few dilapidated mobile homes. Most of them had tires on the rusted sheet metal roof for which I could only assume was to either store the tires or maybe to hold the roof down in high winds. Moccasin Flats. It was here. It was everywhere. Throughout the Rocky Mountains and Sierras. Anywhere you found native Americans in their own private enclave where you are better off driving through. No stopping here, either out of respect or safety.

On this particular trip, after passing miles and miles of these homes and lots more rocks, I slowed down and saw two Native Americans, both in jeans, and both wearing leather boots NOT polished and vests. One had a Stetson hat and the other had a "Cat" Diesel hat. Both had their long black hair braided, I remember that.

There they stood, driving golf balls out into the rocky distance. No country club. No driving range. Just these two guys that seemed happy enough driving golf balls. I wasn't brave enough to stop and interrupt them. I respected their privacy and they probably would not have wanted some dumb city type poking his nose into something that was obviously none of my business. But I still wondered.

There were really no barns on this drive, but everything I saw made me wonder about a story that may be there. Just maybe.

Over the years I have found that people are basically friendly and that most all of them seem to be worth knowing.

Some for a moment and some for a lifetime.

Introduction

This book was inspired by a characteristic that a lot of us have and a few of us act upon. I am nosey. I want to know everything about anything. How it's made, why it was done, who cared about it, all the things that you usually do not find in the history books, but trivia books are full of. My wife and I, now both retired, have a penchant for finding things out. Pat, for research purposes in her career as an attorney, and me, well, like I said, I'm nosey.

Pat and I have been married for 47 years so far and we still like to do things together and sometimes we like to be by ourselves. Sometimes I will take off on my own, and sometimes Pat will accompany me. There really is no rhyme nor reason, just as random events occur, we go together or alone.

This is the plan and pattern for this book; no long range plans, just last minute decisions. The vehicle of choice here was my own 2004 Toyota Sequoia LTD. I purchased it new after my last SUV, a Durango with less than 60 thousand miles on it's odometer needed a serpentine belt replaced. I always bought the added 100,000 mile warranties on all of my vehicles, whether it was my own personal vehicle or it was part of my fleet for my service engineers to use.

I was surprised to hear that although I had a full warranty, that this particular part was not covered and I was going to have to pay over $1200 for it. I had the reigns now, I said park it over there, I'm going to trade it in. One of my employee's cars had impressed me at some point when he picked me up in a 10 year old Toyota. I was very surprised when I closed the door and was rewarded with a solid thud, just like that of a brand new car (of the big 3). Turns out Toyota makes one of the most solid cars and were known for their reliability and ability to maintain their resale value. Well, the dealer that sold me my Durango had also started selling Toyotas so I walked over to my favorite salesman up there and within an hour, I drove off with a brand new 2004 Toyota Sequoia LTD WITH a full 100,000 mile warranty that included everything, yes, the serpentine belt too. I have loved that vehicle and here it is, soon to be 2025 and I STILL own it. This is not a plug for Toyota or a slam against the American car industry, it's just my own choice. What I like about this country. Its freedom.

CHAPTER 1

Lost love and the Model T

*S*lowing down, I saw a rusting mailbox mounted on what looked like an old tree branch sticking out of the ground, a frustrated repair after some late-night mischief or maybe a drunk had run down the original. There were no markings on the box, but this was about 5 miles down Roth Creek Road and there didn't seem to be any signs of any other civilization. This was a gravel road that seemed to fit the description: "Turn off the State Road at the filling station and head towards the big hill. Head east until you get to the boat ramp at Roth Creek and go left out of the parking lot. That will be Roth Creek Road. Go about 5 miles and you will see a lone mailbox on the right side. That's "KING FARM". Turn there and follow it back to the widow's house."

Well, here we go. Lots of dust for a humid spring morning. The trees and grass still had some dew left in the spotty shade and the smell of a recently plowed field hung thick in the air. You could tell that this once was a fairly large family farm that had weathered more than its share of history. World War? Civil War? Depression? The old trees that once lined this drive were almost all gone, but still, you could see the outline of the estate. What trees that were left had vines and other signs of years of neglect.

Finally the house came into view; the road swung around a small algae-covered pond north of the house and skirted an overgrown horse pasture that spread up the hill to the house. Typical of the scene, the fence around the pasture had more missing pieces than anything that could resemble a fence. I could now see the barn and a few other out buildings, but decided to go straight to the house and introduce myself.

Cindy was the first to greet me. She was a chocolate lab that showed her age as she lumbered towards the car to investigate this intrusion into her morning nap time. I petted her from the safety of the open window of my car and when we were both satisfied that neither could nor would do any harm, we each went about our business with only a casual eye on the other….you know, just in case. There were a few chickens pecking around the ground and a peacock! strutting around displaying his full plume of feathers, like an older Vaudeville star who still had the ability, just no audience. I saw a few goats in a corral next to the barn, for all the good it did…. One was pulling at the latch on the gate while another one was standing on top of the shed, and just jumped off the roof to the freedom of the yard now. The dog didn't care, so neither did I.

The old banjo player in the bluegrass group the night before had told me about Inez and her family. It's a known fact around here that if you can get a local banjo picker talking about something he knows about (or doesn't), he can lead you on a trip around the world. Since I only wanted to go another county or two over, this was easy pickins. "She has a treasure in that barn of hers" he said, "I have seen it myself. That car is nothing you'd just as soon think twice about. If you get her to tell you the story behind it, well, it just might hold your attention for a bit, just you watch her face as she tells it." I watched his face as he told me this and I could tell that there might be something worth seeing. I'd like to say that I made an early night of it, but I'd be lying. I have never made an early night of it when it comes to talking to another musician, even if he was a banjo player.

I bought another round and then Joe, he's the banjo player, he bought a round. It went on like this for the rest of the night and into the morning. Never knew a banjo player who was so eager to part with his own money matching drink for drink. Joe was one hell of a picker and could sure as hell hold his liquor!

The farm house was situated on the top of a small hill. It was a large Victorian style built, in, if I were to guess, the late 1800's. A steep gabled roof was protected by two turrets on either side with a broken wind vane on the right side. The porch ran around the whole front of the house and down each side, although its supporting role now seemed to be for storage of assorted "stuff". Lots of gingerbread, cornices and finials if you know what those are. I didn't but soon learned. The paint had all but worn away and what must have been fairly bright colors had now faded into a grey obscurity. All in all this seemed to be a fairly substantial home for its time. As I turned to look down the drive that I had just come up, I noticed two stone pillars, or piles that once were pillars as the road came out of the tree-lined drive. I hadn't seen these on the way up but from here I could see an ornate, hand wrought, iron sign that must have, at one time, hung between the stone pillars. Through the rust and broken letters

I could make out the words "KÖNIG FARM" (KÖNIG is German for KING) as it should be hanging as a welcome and proclamation to all who entered.

I must have heard someone clear their throat as I turned and met Inez. She was just as described; a tall, slender, woman, with grey hair pulled into a ponytail, still attractive for her age at 74. She wore a faded, floral print house dress with a buttoned starched collar. I introduced myself and after we exchanged some pleasantries, I started my pitch.

"You see," I began, "I started off on a road trip to find interesting stories in these old barns that dot the state with the intent of turning a collection of them into a book. Not a travel guide, but just some lost and forgotten Americana and tradition before the next generation takes over and they are forgotten forever." This last sentence seemed to have made her stop to think about it as it seemed to just hang in the air. I could tell she was thinking about it; as Joe had said: Her face tells tales.

I began again; "Our stay in town last night led me to meet up with a chatty banjo player named…." She stopped me right there by putting up her hand as if she had finished listening, but to my surprise, continued my sentence with "That useless banjo player Joe Hubbard" while shaking her head in the usually accepted side to side movement of disagreement or regret.

"Well, there's a story in there," she said, nodding towards the barn. I'm pretty busy these days, so let me think about it. "Call me tomorrow and I'll let you know."

I could tell that this woman had been making decisions on her own for quite some time and she must have learned long ago not to jump at anything unless she absolutely knew and understood all the factors, real OR imagined.

We then agreed that she would call ME in the morning, tomorrow before 7 am, so I gave her my cell number and headed out to the radio blasting Robert Earl Keen's *The Road Goes on Forever and the Party Never Ends.*

Making mental notes as I drove back through the gravel road, the creek road, the boat ramp and finally the left onto the State Road, I found myself once again heading in the wrong direction.

Inez and Harlan owned that farm for as long as Joe knew them. Inez took over the farm after her parents died and her brothers and sisters, there were 6 all together, moved on. She married Harlan Fischer in 1961. Both of them right out of high school. As was customary, the church wedding was had and the reception which followed at the Farmers Co-Op Town Hall was decorated by the local ladies club and all of Inez and Harlan's family and friends. Everyone from town was invited. They had a local band play, which you might have expected music with a country twang to it, but you would be corrected as I was. It turns out this part of Illinois is very proud of it's German heritage and because of that, the Schottische and the Polka are the favored dances of choice around these parts. Now don't get me wrong, there were a few country songs in the set lists but German polkas and the like were celebrated along with Wiener Schnitzel, sauerkraut and any and all types of German and Austrian pastries you can imagine. Did I mention that they had bier and wine?

My cell phone thundered into my aching head just before seven. Inez was nothing if not prompt. She told me she had thought long and hard through the night, and had concluded that the story should be told. She didn't want it to fade away, it had too much significance to her. We agreed that if I would return to King Farms, then she would put on the coffee.

I was again greeted by the now friendly lab, and she accompanied me to the porch. Apparently Cindy was a puppy that Inez found in the cinder pile from the old coal-fired furnace that heated the house dating back to the 1930's. No sign of her mother or any other history. Speculation has it that she must have been dropped off by the side of the road and made it just that far.

Inez was ready at the door, and led me into her large inviting kitchen. She took a seat at the well-worn old table, and pointed to the chair next to her. I obediently sat. Her face turned to gaze out the window to the barn, and her eyes took on a mixture of sadness and remembrance. Her mouth turned up into a small smile. I waited, I could tell she was thinking of things that were well back in her memory.

Finally, she said "I guess I'll begin where my mama did. I was about 4 years old when I first saw the car in the barn. Mama knew that I was too young to understand much about the importance of family history right then, so she just told me that it was a 1917 Ford Model T, and had been my grandfather, Noah Pfluger's pride. As I got older, I started asking questions."

As I listened to Inez, I could tell from that beautiful, mixed look in her eyes that this was going to be a long, sad story. I let her tell it her way, not having the heart to interrupt.

"But *why* is that old car here, mama? I asked over and over. Mama would always look sad when I asked, but I couldn't help myself. After a couple of years, my curiosity got to the point where I had to find out. One day, when mama was in town, I got up the nerve to explore the car. I got in on the passenger side, and noticed a box sitting on the floor. I opened it slowly, no idea what might be in it. There were papers, with a lot of writing on them. I was too young to read at that point, and only knew somehow these papers would answer my questions."

She took a long pause. Finally, she said, "well, why don't we go on out there and you can have a look for yourself."

When we entered the old barn, I saw a lot of old tools and rusty farm equipment. But towards the back stood that 1917 Ford. It had a tarp over it and was up on blocks. I helped her pull the tarp over and off. A rusty patina had settled over it these last several decades. Inez began her story again.

"When mama came home, I told her I had looked in the car. She gave me one of her 'you're gonna get it now, girl' looks, but then her face changed to a kind of resigned understanding. She knew I had to know.

My grandfather bought it right off the showroom floor in 1917. He told my grandma that it would be her wedding present, his way of proposing. Grandma didn't think it was much of a present for her, but she was tickled pink about the proposal. They were so much in love, it hurt. So, Plans were that they soon were quickly married at the Catholic in town, a small ceremony. It had to be, because grandfather had just decided that he was going into the Army. America had entered The Great War, the Yanks were coming. They only had two weeks together before he left for Columbus Barracks Ohio. After training, he went to France as part of The AEF (American Expeditionary Force) under General Pershing's Command, but grandma later found out that he was then sent from France to Belgium. Those papers in that box are letters. Letters to grandma. They really tell the story better than I can."

She pulled the tarp back and motioned to the front seat. I saw the box. I reached for it after making certain that was what she wanted. It was brown and brittle now. It may have been a light green and white sort of leaf print but it just seemed all brown and gray at this point. It had been taped together more than once. I couldn't help but wonder how it could be so important to be repaired and yet still wind up back here on the floor of an old car each time, but that's one mystery that will remain. I can only imagine that it just belongs there.

I walked over to a ray of sunshine breaking its way through the old barn's roof as a few gnats, flies and dust particles took their turn in the natural spotlight before I stepped into that light. I opened the lid of the box and saw that the letters were all mostly still in their original envelopes.

I started to thumb through the papers. Inez put her hand on mine to stop me. She said, "you are welcome to take these up to the house and read through them there. I cannot let them off of the farm, but you can come up and read them anytime you want. When you are finished, we'll just put them back where they belong." This seemed like a workable solution so off we went back to the house.

I began looking through the papers again. Inez had cleared off the dining room table so that I could spread out the treasure that this box held. I noticed, not too far down, that there was a set of letters that had an old, faded pink ribbon around them.

These were Noahs's letters to Anna.

His love letters.

I felt odd holding them, knowing that these were the intimate thoughts placed on paper for Noah's only love.

Not for me.

Not for anyone, except *his* love.

I took a walk around the farm, avoiding Inez so that I might try and work out my dilemma. I made it down to the pond and tried to skip a rock or two, but the algae covering or my lack of talents cancelled that. I decided to continue my walk and came upon an old hickory tree that must have been taken down in a storm a few years back. It was one of many in this stand of trees, but it was right on the edge. There had seemed to be some activity years ago because the trunk had been stripped of its branches and had been cut into 24 inch logs. There was also a pile of split wood already started into a stack. It didn't take too much looking until I stumbled across an old maul and a wedge. Both had their share of rust, but just looking at the mushroomed head on the wedge, you could tell this was at least a hundred years old. Wasn't long before I was back to splitting wood, one of my favorite past-times to clear my head. Since this tree was already seasoned, it was short work for me to get more than a rack of firewood split and stacked.

Even in the cool spring air I was soaked with perspiration. I stretched out on the long grass that I had been walking on and soon saw Inez standing above me with a glass of lemonade. She took a drink...It wasn't for me. Then, with a little smile she motioned over to the stack where she had placed mine.

"You don't need to do that," she said, "But I do appreciate it. You give up already?"

"I got about half a cord already!" I protested.

"No, I was talking about the letters." She said.

"Oh," I said, brushing off my pants as I stood. I explained that I was feeling uncomfortable about going through someone's most private thoughts. Inez said that she understood my feelings, but drug me right back to my opening pitch: "Just some lost and forgotten Americana and tradition before the next generation takes over and they are forgotten forever. That's what you said as a statement of fact. Nothing more and nothing less" as she then stood staring at me, just waiting for a "But…."

I have been alive long enough to know that when a woman uses your own words in an argument, you have little chance of coming back from that precipice. "Let's go back to the house and maybe I can help," she said.

When we got back to the house, Inez sat me in the same chair and made sure I had a fresh cup of coffee before she was called back outside to tend to her chickens.

"We regret to inform you that your husband, Noah Friedrich Pfluger was assumed Missing in Action on the 11th of November, 1918 during the Ypres-Lys campaign"

This was the letter that was on the top in the box. Very concise. To the point. I could only imagine what someone; a wife, a mother, a father, a daughter, might feel upon opening this. Although I did not know this family and had really just met the matriarch, a lump rose in my throat and my eyes began to water. I was attached to them. In just this short little time, a bond had grown. I didn't start out for it to happen, and I certainly never expected this. Here I am doing research for the very first story for my book and I am so greatly affected. How will I go on? Do I even want to? This is going to be a very emotional project and I am not sure that I am up to it.

I decided to start at the beginning and went to the bottom of the box. A complimentary ticket stub from some tractor show. A pressed penny from a state fair. A blue ribbon for first prize in a school spelling bee; I am not sure of the year or even whose it was. I will assume it was Noah's.

It seems that Noah had met Anna Konig in grade school that they both attended as required by the county. In speaking with Inez, Anna, her grandmother was quite a student and was at the top of her class every year. At some point, Noah Pfluger became a contender for the top spot and soon they were competing against each other in the science fairs, spelling bee, and even for the top spot in the Regional 4 H Club. It was uncommon for many school-aged children to continue their education much after 6th grade while being raised on a farm. A few made it through 8th grade, all in the same one-room school house I understand. Anna was different. She came from a substantial farming family. They recognized the talent and intellect that she had and were proud to let her continue with her schooling…..as long as it didn't interfere with her chores.

As fate would have it, Noah's father, the local mechanic who sometimes took jobs with the local Case Farm Tractor dealer, recognized his son's talents and skills as well. Noah Pfluger's father's name was Abe Pfluger and sometime around the turn of the 20th century, so impressed the local Agricultural Equipment dealer that he was made a partner in the dealership. He soon realized that sales was an exceptional way to provide for his family and sold off his meager family farm and livestock. From what Inez remembered, the family soon had a large house on the main street in town and Noah was expected to go to school and earn his high school diploma, which he did.

Through elementary school and high school Noah and Anna became best friends, worst enemies and constant competitors. Sometime in their sophomore year, they began seeing one another as more than friends. It seems their parents were now in the same social circles and were together many times a month. Inez told of the first time that Noah kissed Anna, as retold to her by her mother. It was their third official date, and they had gone to the local farm implement show at the local fairgrounds. Anna was a little more forward than Noah and she was wondering why he hadn't ever tried to hold her hand, much less kiss her. She had decided that she would ask Noah directly. "He should be able to answer a few yes or no questions" Inez remarked as she stared me down once again.

As they ever so slowly walked towards her home, Noah walked closer and closer to her. Eventually their arms brushed a few times. Anna's heart started racing. They were looking straight ahead as they walked. Soon their fingers were lightly brushing against each other as their arms swung in the summer heat. And then it happened, with the little finger of her left hand, she hooked Noah's little finger of his right hand. Although they kept on walking, Anna seemed to be walking a bit higher, almost floating.

Still walking and looking straight ahead, she didn't notice her heart racing any longer, but began to smile. After they had passed the dry goods store and the butcher shop, she turned to look at Noah and he was smiling too, still looking straight ahead. Inez said that her mama ended the story there, but she had many dreams about their happiness as she was falling asleep thinking about that 1917 Model T Ford.......I know, it wasn't the car.

There were a few letters from Noah to Anna, written over the next few years. Mostly when Noah went on vacation with his family (really a tractor convention up in Racine Wisconsin). He liked the tours through the building and described the tractors and their specifications in great detail, which, although boring to me, had kept Anna's attention for years on end. Noah had his father's gift for mechanics and pursued that in school after this trip. There was one other letter when he was a junior in high school when he became sick with the flu. Although Noah was not stricken that badly and made a full recovery, his mother did not and was buried that same year in the town cemetery. "That was a bad year according to Mama," said Inez. Noah kept close to the house and his father that year. Although they did see each other at school, it was a year before they really got back together.

After they graduated high school in 1917, they both began working more and more. Anna on the family farm and Noah with the family business. Try as he could, Noah could not convince Anna's father Andreas Konig to buy a Case tractor. The plan that they developed in their minds was that if only Andreas would buy a Case tractor from Noah's family, he could be over there all the time taking care of the tractor.....

Inez told me that by now the country was feeling the affects of war, from both overseas with the radio broadcasts and locally with the difficulty in obtaining certain items. All punctuated by the few remaining ration books that were scattered among the letters. As 1917 came into the summer, talk had turned from isolationism to patriotism and when the passenger ships carrying Americans were sunk, well, every young man soon thought of going to war. Noah was no exception and signed up after many discussions with Anna and with his father. Neither wanted him to go, but Noah was resolute and had a strong mind.

The day of his departure at the train station was unremarkable except for the fact that two newlyweds were now parting after only two weeks. Although she promised that she wouldn't cry, she did. Noah kept holding her until the final "All Aboard!" was called, gave her a kiss on the lips and said, "I'll see you soon my love."

The letters came from Noah almost every other day. He apologized for the brevity of his letters as he was so busy with training. There was so much he wanted to tell her of his new encounters and experiences. So much he wanted to share with her about his new friends and what he was learning. The letters were mostly very technical and specific about barracks life and his training at first. As I read through them, I recognized how they were developing and that Noah was realizing what he and the other recruits were about to be called upon to do.

When he got his shipping orders, although he couldn't tell when he would leave or where he might be going, it was assumed that he was heading to France. A few more letters later and he was on a five week troop transport that was in the north Atlantic. Well that narrowed it down to England or France. A few more on board letters found him with a sprained ankle after tripping through a gangway. A day in sick bay and limited walking had him back to new as they docked in Port Saint-Nazaire France.

The next letter Noah describes life in the trenches at the front. After disembarking, the troops were sent to the Meuse-Argonne campaign. Arriving in October, he describes the absolute carnage that is hard to imagine.

No man's land. It is a barren, fog enshrouded hell, with no recognizable features. What was once a fertile land of rolling hills and valleys covered in trees and pastures, is now a land burned, black and brown. Barbed wire criss-crossing barricades, shell holes still smoldering hours or even days later.

There are trenches here that men must live in, no, they must survive in them. Some knee deep with filthy, reddish brown water unfit for animal consumption, much less human. But this place isn't human. Where there is no water, there is mud. Always ankle deep and sometimes knee deep. The smell is too putrid to describe. Yes there has been death here. A lot of it, and you soon find yourself not looking at anything for fear of seeing a finger, an ear, a toe. The medical corps does a very good job of tending to the injured and the dead, but they just cannot stop and find every last piece of a body. Noah was describing not his first day here, but what seemed to be after a few months.

He said that they did get rotated in and out on a somewhat regular basis, but it was always the same once they were sent back. And not even to the same place. Hell, a soldier could have come back to the same place 2 weeks later.....he would never know it. The only thing that they could count on was the constant shelling, the constant gun fire.

By this time Noah had seen more than his share and was trying NOT to describe what he was living through. In one letter, he was wildly excited by the news that Anna was going to have a baby, maybe sometime in March 1918! That news buoyed him from the depths of this mire and his next half dozen letters go on about what to name the baby and where they might live when he returns. Anna was living on the farm with her parents and the rest of her brothers and sisters. Anna and her father picked out a nice little piece of land on the property of the Konig Farm and were planning a house for them. Noah seemed fine with this plan and asked if there could be a garage attached to the house so that they could park his new car inside and that would keep her and the baby from having to deal with all this snow, water and rain that we are having here. The Meuse-Argonne Campaign must be horrible, Anna thought.

The next letter apprised Anna that Noah was on the move again. This time they were trying to stop the Huns' drive to the sea. The Germans were in Belgium and now pushing towards the North Sea. They must be stopped, so Noah and the 37th Infantry Division were being sent across the border and into Belgium. Another couple of letters as they were being transported and sidetracked and then back on the trail again. Soon Noah was in a trench in an area of Belgium known for the Ypres-Lys Offensive. The Brits all pronounced it *wipers.* Again he was writing in a trench, squatting in an uncomfortable, crouched position with his feet in a mixture of water, blood and mud. It was a short letter.

That was the last letter Anna received from Noah.

Now, I picked up another official looking letter, addressed to Anna. This one was hand-written, from a Lieutenant Fitzgerald on October 30 1918. As he starts, it seems that he was the only one left to write this letter because their captain and rest of the officers were injured or outright killed in the campaign. Lt. Fitzgerald said that he gotten to know Noah and began speaking to him often in the trenches as he did his routine inspections.

Noah was a very friendly and talkative private who knew that he had a job to do, all the while cursing the war. *"One day he offered me a cigarette as I passed him. I turned and was about to lecture him on the priorities and duties of an officer, but when I saw the look on his face, innocence, confusion and a bit of fright, I rethought my decision. In this war you really don't want to make friends, they can be gone in an instant. I learned about you and the expected child that afternoon. I learned about the farm and southern Illinois. He described everything so colorfully…..From my experiences growing up in Newark New Jersey, I was thoroughly entranced as he spoke of the tree lined drive, the grass pasture in front and the pond at the bottom of the hill in front of your house. It sounds wonderful. By this time I am certain that by now you know that he has been missing but we are doing everything we can to locate him or any sign of him. There are a lot of trenches and holes that he could be in or he may have hooked up with another division and gone somewhere else. Please do not give up hope for him. Sometimes out here hope is all we have, and knowing someone is waiting for us, well, it may seem small to you but to some of us, it's the reason we fight. We will not give up."*

Anna did not give up hope. She researched everything there was to know about the final battle of Ypres-Lys of 1918 and although she wrote to and subsequently met quite a few people who knew her beloved Noah, none had positive information as to his final whereabouts. Her thoughts often drifted back to that day at the train station, the last time she saw him, the last time she touched him, the last time she kissed him, the last time she smelled him, the last time she felt him.......the last time.

Anna gave birth to Amelia Pfluger in March of 1918. She told her the story of her father over and over. One by one Anna's brothers and sisters moved off the farm. Her parents had died in the Spanish Flu of 1918. Anna raised Amelia and Amelia fell in love with Benjamin Becker and married him in 1936. Anna died in 1962 . Amelia and Benjamin had 5 other children, who, one by one, left the farm life for something better in the big city. All but Inez. She stayed and married Harlan Fischer in 1961. Her children also had no love for the farm and also left to find their fortune, fame or solitude.

The Car. It was cherished by each and every one of the children from Amelia on down. Each wanted to hear the story. Each has their own version of it. Each of the boys took their turn at starting it and getting it running again as some sort of tribute while each of the girls sometimes cried themselves to sleep at night thinking about romance and what could have been.

And Anna. Anna died with the solitary consoling thought that somewhere in Flanders Field, her Noah is waiting for her.

CHAPTER 2

Even a Blind Farmer Finds an Avery Once in Awhile

Yesterday Pat and I went to the Greenville Steam and Agricultural tractor exhibit. I have always been a fan of older machinery. Watching a piece of iron over 100 years old still operating and sometimes even continuing the duty that it was originally built for still brings a smile to my face. With today's throw-away society, standing next to a machine with a 15 foot tall smoke stack sticking out from a boiler you could drive a small car under is awe inspiring to say the least.

I caught the bug for live steam when we took our kids to Branson Missouri in the 1980's for the Silver Dollar City Crafts Festival. Now you may think of crocheted pot holders and hand carved trinkets but you would be wrong. This festival was to acquaint everyone with life before the Industrial Age. A time when our relatives and ancestors were setting off to find their fortune and make their mark in the world.

My own ancestors came from Germany in the 1860's and settled in southern Illinois in Ashley and Radom, Illinois. I don't know if they had any steam engines, as they had large families, small farms and little affinity for farm life. One by one they wound up in the St. Louis area. I saw first hand how they may have lived back then during these trips to southwestern Missouri.

During the festivals in Branson, they tried to reconstruct the farm community from that era. They wanted to show how people had developed to make their lives more productive and successful in the 1800s. Some of my long-standing memories of these trips were the sounds and the smells. Live steam engines of that time were usually powered by coal. Except on the farm, you had no coal. What you did have however, was a lot of trees. So the smell permeating the festival was of hardwood, usually oak, burning for the engines, with the hickory saved for cooking to impart that wonderful smoke flavor to the meats. Live steam engines were brought to Silver Dollar City for the festival and demonstrated how they were used, not to plow fields, but to cut lumber, thresh grain, grind sorghum and just about anything else you might need a team of horses or the backs of men to accomplish. Why one time, I watched a stationary steam tractor power a woodworking shop to actually turn rifle stocks on what was called a repeating lathe. Now if you look at a wooden rifle stock, and then look at a lathe from your days in high school shop class, you may not see the connection as to how that would even be accomplished. With a template and guide bar, the intricate cuts and curves are followed and reproduced exactly each and every time.

The last craft festival that we attended did indeed have the live steam engines, but they are all now powered with a diesel-fired boiler. The whole place now smells like it just had a fresh coating of asphalt applied. Not at all conducive to my memory.

Back in Greenville that Sunday afternoon, one of the steam tractors that was being exhibited was unattended while we were there. There were a lot of things to see and we enjoyed a show by an all female bluegrass band called the Pickin' Chicks, that was quite good. The food was also a treat as were the old tractor pulls with the steam tractors as usual, pulling the winners of the internal combustion class across the finish line every time.

Bruce Vogt and his family were the owners of a 1909 Avery Company 65 HP straight flue steam traction engine. At least that's what the placard in front of the engine said. We kept coming back to that tractor throughout the day, and since it was the last day, I figured that coming back around closing time would work. It was 4:30 when we came back to camp out until we met Bruce or anyone of the Vogt family. About dusk they started arriving and taking down the display and getting ready to move the behemoth onto a flatbed trailer that unmistakably claimed it as Vogt Farms, Ky. I got to talk briefly with Bruce after I introduced myself and told him that I would like to learn a little bit more about his tractor and its family legacy, if it did indeed have one. Bruce assured me that "Yes, my grandfather bought this tractor for his farm in Kentucky after the family settled there from Europe." He was evidently very busy trying to get this loaded and I asked if I might stop by sometime and talk to him about it. He said that they were headed back home in the morning. It would be late by the time everything was lashed down and ready to go, so they were staying in the RV, but we were welcome to find a motel in town and follow them back home tomorrow. It was agreed to meet back there at 5 AM and we set off to find a motel in this swinging town. There were a couple of rooms available, but they had not been cleaned yet, so off we went down the road in search of a motel, not too far away. Keep in mind a 5 AM meet up means getting up, checking out and gassing up a lot earlier than 5 AM!

Well, we made it. Bruce and his group were busy with last minute details and permits to move this hunk of iron down the interstate into Kentucky. We had a cup of coffee while they went over the route with the pilot car. Bruce handed me a hand-drawn map to use once we got off the interstate. He suggested that it would be after noon when we got into Kentucky. That is where we should get off the highway to find some lunch and spend a couple of hours doing something other than being in their way when they all got home. Seemed like good advice.

We followed the caravan threading through the mostly flat Illinois interstate system and dutifully honked and waved as we left the interstate in downtown Paducah Kentucky. Downtown Paducah has a beautiful waterfront which I have been able to see from both the land side as well as the water side. Although I had no formal introduction to water, I remember being tossed into a 4ft deep swimming pool when I was about 4 years old by the father. I didn't learn to swim from that experience. No, I was sent to swimming lessons after my mother saw that and eventually learned to swim with the help from the Red Cross. I went on to get my Lifesaving Certificate and when I hit 16, I was able to get a job at a local apartment complex. A nice gig for a high school teenager when all the other jobs seemed to have something to do with deep fried fast food or shoveling something or other at a back breaking pace. No, I recommend going the lifesaving route. It offered very little to do as for hard work, a nice tan and the girls seemed to like lifeguard's chlorine scented cologne better than the fried food essence left from a shift at Micky D's. From there I found out about boating and the fun it offered. Pat and I got the boating bug soon after we were married and went from sail boat, to runabout to cruiser to larger crusier. From there we often came from St. Louis down to Kentucky Kake. I bring all of this up because as we were sitting at DOE'S EAT on the Paducah Riverwalk, we could reminisce our trips up the Ohio and up the Tennessee River right there in front of us! Well, we make it a point to stop in here when we are anywhere within range. After a great lunch, (I recommend the Grilled Chicken and Pat suggests the Scallops if they have them when you visit,) we were on our way once again. From there the map that he drew was very direct to the farm, and we planned to arrive there around 6 pm, well after they had removed the tractor from its trailer. Following it all those miles, and seeing it strapped and chained down to that flatbed, I couldn't help but think back to my childhood with the View-Master Stereo images of the Lilliputians trying to restrain Gulliver. (You may or may not get this reference.) You just know Gulliver could get up and break those little strings and chains whenever he felt like it. I'm just glad Bruce's Gulliver was happy to nap.

Since we were only about an hour from his place, when I called him I asked if we might come by the next morning, thinking we would get a hotel downtown. "NO WAY!" he exclaimed "We are expecting you for a big dinner with the family tonight. The wife already has the RV cleaned and the bedding changed. You are staying with us tonight." Did I mention that Bruce was a big ol' country boy? Well, he was persuasive and we agreed. We made it to his Kentucky farm by 6 pm and were welcomed like old family.

Gracious hosts that they were, they first showed us to our lodging for the night so that we could unpack and relax a bit before they "sprung" the big family dinner on us…..Bruce's words, not mine. The RV was very luxurious and welcoming. Having travelled the riverways in cabin cruisers for the last 40 years, we were very accustomed to this 'Land Yacht" and we were quite content in its furnishings. Bruce had laid a nice concrete pad with electrical, water and sewer hook ups so this could be used as a guest cabin any time they needed it. Bruce also told me it was a nice respite from the family drama when needed. I could only nod in agreement.

As instructed, once we were settled in the RV we didn't bother knocking on the front door, but just walked right in. This farm house was a large authentic home from the mid 1800's I would guess. The home was two stories tall with two dormers gracing the southerly-facing facade. A wrap-around porch offered at least one swing and one rocking chair on each side. Although the house was originally a square shape when Bruce's great-grandfather built it, with the continued growth of a farm family, additions had changed its shape that the now serpentined porch followed. Although not an architect, the original Mr. Vogt certainly had an eye for detail. Knowing that there were at least four different additions built onto this frame, you would still be tasked to see where the old one stopped and the new one started. He even brought the first electrical lines in from the new towers of the TVA when it first came into being. The word was that Bruce's father, following his fathers instructions, brought the home up to modern-day standards as it developed, each taking care to respect the design of the other. Bruce showed me a book that the original owner, Mr. Nicholas Vogt, brought from Alsaise-Lorraine on the design, structure and building of this home. It had been carefully added to over the years, and now was three volumes, the last brought up to date in the 1960s by Bruce's father, Paul Vogt.

As fate would have it, they had a nicely restored 1972 Baldwin Grand Piano in a polished ebony. It turns out that I was not the only musician in this room. At Bruce's suggestion, Sue sat down and the piano and begin playing for us. After a warm up of Beethoven's "Fur Elise", Sue then asked if there were anything we would like to hear. Well, I turned it back to her and said, please play something for us. And with this, she started playing some pieces from Phantom Of the Opera, as she had heard over dinner that I had seen the broadway show more than 10 times. We all sat quietly while she played many of our favorites. It turns out their two daughters are singers as well as one of their sons who joined in for the finale with "All I Ask Of You"! WOW! It was almost like having a front row at the MET!

Since they were such gracious hosts, Sue then very professionally stood and introduced me as a special guest soloist!??!?"?" I had nothing prepared. BUT, as a musician, I always had something prepared and went into some barrelhouse Boogie Woogie which did not call up any of my vocal (in)abilities. Soon Bruce and Sue were up cutting up the rug until I could play no more. Boogie Woogie is hard work on a piano pounder if you are not in practice.

A warm fall evening was unfolding before us as well as the fantastic meal that we were about to partake in. After casually being introduced to the rest of the family and some we had already met back in Greenville, we had a cocktail and some interesting stories before we sat down at the table and broke bread this Sunday evening. We learned that Bruce and Sue Vogt are the third generation Vogts to run this farm in southwestern Kentucky. Bruce's wife Sue was born Neikemper and learned her mother's flair for cooking. This Sunday night's meal would include fried chicken, schnitzel, a mixture of German sausages that come from the farm's own pork and beef, spaetzle, potato salad, bean salad and an assortment of home-baked breads. Turns out that they had called ahead and told their oldest daughter, who lived on the "compound" a few "holler's" over, that they were bringing home some "strays", as Bruce called us, and to get ready to prepare a big dinner. Patty, the oldest daughter, just happened to be baking bread for the week and didn't have anything else to do, other than run her farm and raise her family. She was very sweet about it and really enjoys her parents and their "strays".

As the dinner progressed the discussion got around to my book and although they were very interested in the story lines, I could tell a lot of them thought that this may be a little more exposure than the family wanted. I assured them that everything would be kept as anonymous as could be since this was going to be classified as fiction anyway. I even agreed to let them each read this chapter and offer any additions or deletions that they might have. And that is how we got to research the Vogt family immigration to the United States of America in the fall of 1883.

Nicholas Vogt boarded a German steamship as a carpenter for passage to the New World. Born in the Alsaise-Lorraine area of either Germany or France, (depending on who won the last war or who was telling the story - To this day, the Vogt family is STILL arguing it and there are some staunch hold-outs on either side.) Nicholas had substantial savings that his family generously added to. His mother and father were excited about the prospect of "free land" which they had been reading about since the Homestead Act of 1863 had been passed by the US Government. Nicholas, however, pressed back that he could rely on his carpentry skill. He landed at Castle Garden Depot, predecessor to Ellis Island in New York, and quickly decided that he didn't particularly like the east coast of the USA and, as he had read about new building growth further west, he managed to get to Philadelphia via rail. Spending a few months in Philly, the wanderlust still fresh, he learned a bit more of the language and booked a straight back seat on the Pennsylvania Railroad to Chicago Illinois. Slowly pulling into Chicago, past the stock yards and some of the seedier parts of Chicago's south side, Nicholas always remembered the experience was much like walking past a group of people who all had turned their backs towards you. Not a welcoming sight at all.

Arriving at Union Station in downtown Chicago, the city looked to be just what he was searching for. The landscape in Chicago was ready for a building boom as real estate and other properties were in high demand. So were workers. A union card would be required before he would be allowed to work. It turned out that although there were many carpentry jobs to be had at this time in Chicago's history, you had to know someone or have someone vouch for you in order to find meaningful work. He was getting by on piece-work jobs at local factories and although he had the skills, he was not known and since there was no union card, he was still blocked from the start of his dreams. Apparently during these times, he had earned enough money to afford himself a nice room or apartment in the "German Section of Chicago", again the family is split on this point and I believed that the story might change at some time during this night as the beer and other libations greased the wheels, if you know what

I mean. From what I could tell, he held onto his savings while living off of his wages.

Theresa Marie Carlsburg met Nicholas Johannes Vogt in the Spring of 1884 and they were married on Christmas Day 1885 at Chicago City Hall, after paying the required fees, licenses and payoffs to the local politicians. The wedding was nothing impressive enough to garner even a small announcement in the Chicago Tribune. Her parent had save a bit for the wedding of their only daughter, but, Theresa convinced her parents that a small wedding would be fine and that she would really rather have the money for their future. Parents of any child love to hear this talk and they were all happy with the small wedding at City Hall with family and a few friends attending a small meal and toasts afterwards. What a beautiful start to their lives together. The couple was frugal and saved their money as best they could. Theresa worked as a typist in one of the downtown law firms, only after having assured the hiring managers that she was unmarried and living at a proper young ladies' boarding house. All was going well for the young couple. They were making friends and his carpentry work was in high demand. There was talk on the job about his boss recommending him to the local carpenters union at the time. The commute to work for Theresa was a far distance, as the "L" had not yet been built, but she was able to be at work a half hour early every day and she made it a point to stay after work every evening. The brisk walk against the fierce winds of downtown Chicago always kept her watching for any path that may take her out of the force of the winds. The spring and summer were her favorite times. She also secretly loved the winter as any spare time that she had was spent snuggled up in their huge bed with over stuffed pillows and TWO comforters, a concession she made sure that she had BEFORE they were married. This allowed her ample time to read and improve her English so that no one could detect anything but a very slight accent, which even then, was almost undetectable except from anyone with a trained ear in linguistics.

Nicholas was used to calls coming at all times of the night for window board up or odd jobs as they would occur to his boss. One particular night, a courier sent by his boss found him just before he got home and told him to get down to the new job site. Nicholas and Stosh had become close friends since they had seen each other at the union hall. Stosh said he would go with him, but Nicholas asked him to just tell Theresa to that he would be a little late getting home. The courier could only tell him that there was trouble. It seems that there were some union "thugs" picketing the job site and things were looking to get out of hand. Nicholas ran the back alleys and streets as fast as he could. When he turned the corner from South Cicero to the job site, he saw what he later described as a total riot with lots of men swinging fists, boards and any tool that they thought would give them an edge over their opponent. He remembered that the police just seemed to stand there and were not trying to stop any of the violence. He saw pro-union men telling the others that they were not allowed to work there and he saw others, who just wanted to work, trying to stand up for their rights as free men. Then it happened.

At this point the story all the family will agree that it must have been picked up by Nicholas's wife, Theresa, as she was awakened by Nicholas's boss pounding on the door to their apartment. It seems that there was an awful accident and that Nicholas was in the hospital. He took her to be by his side in an early morning carriage ride to Mercy Hospital. Stosh was in the carriage with them. They arrived at the hospital and it was chaos. And this was a normal day. There she found Nicholas was being treated for a head wound. She was being shoved and moved and asked questions she had no answers to. She was moved from waiting room to waiting room, each seems to be filled with many loud and brusk people with no manners whatsoever. Stosh helped her get through this, but soon he too had to leave for work. Hours passed before a doctor and nurse told her that her husband had suffered a blow to the head, which she already knew. From what they could tell, he had been kneeling on the ground and someone had hit him from above with a hammer. He had been brought here by a friend, they told her. That would be Stosh she said, perhaps he could give them the information they were asking about. After a time, they decided that the information needed was not that necessary at all. Stosh would show up and sit with her and hold her had and tell her all would be fine. He pressed as he could to get more information, but whenever he gave them information, it seemed to make no difference and just resulted in more and more questions to be unleashed. Theresa could not get in to see him for several days. Apparently there was not much to do for a head wound of that nature in those days. Hope and pray is what they told her.....and *that* she did. When she finally was allowed entry to see him, she was not prepared for the sight. His head was bandaged, his face was bruised and scraped, and both of his hands were bandaged. There were traces of blood seeping through the gauze bandages which gave her at least a *little* cause to question their abilities.

It was in the second week that Nicholas finally regained consciousness. He opened his eyes and nothing. He put is hands to his face and began to rub his eyes. That is the way the Nicolas found out that he had been blinded. The optic nerve and its place in the brain are always to be protected and isolated from any shock. It doesn't really take a neurosurgeon to tell you that a trauma to the head such as a hit with a hammer will, if not kill you, leave you either paralyzed or blind.

They assured her that he was getting adequate treatment and everything that could be done, was being done for him. A man who had just had both legs amputated would need a certain amount of nursing that WAIT! WAIT! BOTH LEGS AMPUTATED? WHAT HAVE YOU DONE WITH MY HUSBAND?! I DEMAND TO SEE HIM NOW!! When it was sorted out, he had not had his legs amputated. And if he did, he is in much better hand......She pushed away from this group of people and finally found Stosh at the administration desk. She told him what was said and he grabbed her arm and took her almost running back to the ward where they had last seen Nicholas. There they at least found him in the same condition and much better than someone who had his legs amputated. After catching their breath, and a short discussion to determine that the caregivers here were indeed capable of all human nature and could make mistakes.

Theresa held vigil there through the nights as they turned to days which turned to weeks. Her boss at the time was understanding, due to his anti-union sentiment, and he allowed her to put in hours when she could. Nicholas's boss also agreed to take care of the medical bills for the time being. He also put on Stosh in Nicholas's place so that Stosh could at least help Theresa with much needed emotional and a little financial support.

With Theresa at his side every, every evening they spoke with friends and acquaintances as they would stop in to see him and offer their condolences to them both. From this point, it was pieced together that on the night Nicholas was asked to go to the job site, some anti-union workers and pro-union workers came together and began bullying each other. From what we would be able to tell from the story, Nicholas may have been involved in the fighting, but at this time, his friends made it clear that the violence had settled down and things were cooling off. It seems that Nicholas had bent down to start to pick up some of the boards and materials that had been scattered during the melee. He was on his knees with his hands holding a large timber when someone came up and stomped on the board, probably breaking his hands at that point. With his hands pinned under the timber, and more than a few unintelligible German curse words coming from his mouth, someone came running up behind Nicholas and hit him on the back of the head with a carpenter's hammer. A few shots were fired by the police at that time and the crowd scattered. But it was too late. Some of the workers that knew him carried him to his boss's wagon and they drove him to Mercy Hospital.

Nicholas was discharged and sent back home to Theresa with a white cane and a pair of dark glasses. His hands had healed, and the couple were still together and alive. Stosh would stop in from time to time with news from is friends and work.

Word had reached Germany and Nicholas's family about the dilemma. His mother wanted him to come home immediately. Aunts and uncles, nieces and nephews all wrote and offered their condolences and suggestions. Letters passed forth and back across the Atlantic. Some offered a place to return to. Nicholas and Theresa wanted nothing of that. Some offered suggestions that they push on out to the west and see what would happen. Theresa was sure that it could not get any worse and they both had their own ideas, but soon it was decided that Nick and Theresa would move somewhere south, away from Chicago, and make a life together on a farm. They bought two tickets on the Illinois Central Railway to get them to a place as far from any large city as they could find within reason. The train ride took them through beautiful country which she described to him to every last leaf on every last tree. Every speck of sand and every last pedal of every last flower. Theresa wanted to put everything "bad" behind them. Everything beautiful lay ahead. Leaving Chicago for the land of their dreams. Even if they had yet to have those dreams about this place, Theresa would describe them. At every stop, she would arrange for their luggage to be brought off and sent to each new town that she felt was worthy of a side trip. She would help Nicholas map out the area in his mind with these off trips. Returning to the train the next days or week, would allow them both to learn the land and each other. As he relied on Theresa to be his eyes, she allowed him to be the architect of their future. The beauty of the future was to be captured by them both, but Theresa caught each glimmer, every fleck every flash and turned it into a beautiful picture to a man who could not see. Nicholas grasp at each of these rays of hope that Theresa described to him. He would remember these all of his life to come. This was his new life.

There was a station in Cairo Illinois where they disembarked with all their worldly belongings and took up residence in the only hotel in town. From there, they searched for a suitable farm. It didn't take too long for them to cross the Ohio River via ferry into Kentucky. They found that western Kentucky was as beautiful as the river valleys they had left in their beloved Germany. Theresa would describe the scenery as they would travel the local roads and they would talk about the old country and between the two of them, they found a rekindled love between themselves and the country. They decided to settle there. Somewhere the farming life came back to both of them from their childhoods. Nick and Theresa must have amassed a small fortune, or else they brought it with them from the old country, or maybe a little of both. At any rate they had a place to stay, a means of support and with the cooperative western Kentucky weather, they became happy enough once again. Hired help was easy to find and sharecropping brought in an added income each season. A blind man was soon able to farm, though limited, they could put him behind the plow and with a little luck the rows would end up straight enough. Two children came soon after. Norbert Vogt was born in 1888. A daughter, whom they named Johanna was born in 1891. Norbert took the job of big brother very seriously and was very protective of his little sister. It must have been a hard life, but through hard work, they persevered.

Sometime around the second round of coffee and cake, Bruce told me that his father had described Grampa Nick to him as he was back in the 1920's or so. He said that Nick would always be dressed in black. Always. Dark, round gold framed glasses and a white, starched shirt. A long grey full-face beard reached almost to his lap. He did not use a cane at that time, but when he stood, he was every bit of 6 feet tall and still a very formidable man whose broad shoulders were his most unforgettable feature. He spoke very softly when he spoke and you always had to lean in to hear him, unless he was out in the fields or barn. There was no doubt, this man would hold respect when he would talk. His voice although soft when he spoke, commanded attention with not just his volume, but with his vast and awe inspiring outlook on life. As a blind man, many would come to him to ask questions and seek knowledge which he was happy to impart to any and all that came within earshot. And for Nicholas this was also a two way street for he was always eager to learn of his listeners' knowledge and wisdom. Nicholas knew every man had something worthwhile inside either his mind or his heart and Nicholas would do he best to find this and help his friends and neighbors cultivate what he could. For this reason alone, he was often offered a leadership role in whatever project he was around, be it building, laying out acreage for best use as well as the layout of any new towns which seemed to be popping up, it seemed, all over.

As the only son, Bruce's grand-father Norbert took on the burden of farm life at an early age. Norbert stayed on and worked the farm and eventually the property was his after his parents had passed on. His sister died sometime in 1899 from what they believe was the flu. She caught it in November and was buried in December. Sometime in the early 1900's, Bruce thought around 1905, Norbert started looking for a steam tractor to augment his workforce on the homestead. He had investigated many, but after a few visits to some of the regional and local dealers and manufacturers, decided while at the 1906 Iowa State Fair with his father, that the Avery Traction Company of Peoria Illinois would be the best option since it was fairly close and from what he could tell, very reliable. Although it took a few years of correspondence, Norbert traveled to Peoria, Illinois in 1909, signed the agreement and arranged for the money to be wired to the Peoria National Bank. Bruce showed me the paperwork as he had collected as much as he could over the years for this antique.

The tractor was delivered to Cairo by rail and then loaded onto the ferry with great concern that it might be too much weight for the vessel. Everything was fine and according to the records, the fee to cross on the ferry was re-negotiated after the trip. It seems the steel landing that the ferry plowed into each crossing had been pushed very far up the bank so that a number of trees had to be felled to be used to fill in the gap since the weight of the tractor was keeping the landing ramp from reaching the ferry. Nicholas and Norbert saw his first opportunity for this new purchase to "earn its keep". In return for pulling/pushing the entire steel structure back into place for the ferry company, and a day or two pulling stumps and rearranging the logs of the landing, the crossing bill would be negated and all could go on their way.

As there were no trailers or other means of transportation to convey that massive beast to its final destination, Norbert and his father drove the tractor two days to get back to his farm. They took turns standing on the steel floor on each side while the other sat and drove. Yes, a blind man could drive this tractor at the breakneck speed of 2-3 mph with a top or 5 mph! Of course Norbert would be shouting suggestions to his father. They came to a very unique dialogue between the two of them. There was and always will be a bit of pride when it comes to any father and son relationship and as delicate as those may be, some harsh language was agreed to be used ONLY if there was about to be a life altering disturbance in the path of the tractor. They both got back home with the tractor, none the less for wear and each with his own version of a story when the occasional "bump" in the trip occurred. With any newly obtained piece of equipment, the tractor went on to provide many decades of use and work for the family with it occasionally being loaned out to neighbors who were going through tough times during the Depression.

In no time, it seems that Norbert had raised his family and Bruce's father Paul had been born into the community. Paul worked the farm and just as Norbert had added to the house, so did Paul when it became his time to take over in the 1940's. By this time Bruce and his brothers and sisters were coming into their childhoods and all had remembrances of the tractor; some good, (usually the boys) and some bad, (usually the girls) but not always.

Sometime in the 60's or 70's the Avery fell into disrepair and it sat outside the barn when, during its last routine maintenance, it was discovered that the main piston had a crack in it and its connecting rod also was bent enough to cause the entire project to be halted and left there to rust the rest of its life away.

That is, until the early 2000's, at least a few years before the 100th anniversary of this tractor, when Bruce started to entertain the idea of putting it back together. It began as a repair project, but before that was completed, the idea of a complete rebuild began to percolate. Bruce and his family committed in 2005 to completely rebuild and recondition this tractor for its 100th birthday. There were some close calls with deadlines for parts and new castings to be made, but they made it and began entering it in local festivals and fairs. If you have an inclination for mechanics and history, you would do yourself very well to find a local "olden days festival" or what ever it may be called in your vicinity and attend. This is an easy way to actually step back in time and experience what it was like to live in those days. It is very enlightening and as usual, things that you may have taken for granted just this week, may appear very differently to you. I guarantee if you were to take in one of these fairs, the term "Fast forward to today" will explain why Bruce and his family have every reason to smile and be thankful for the time that the Vogt family has spent farming, traveling and letting others see the small bit of history that their family has made and contributed to this small corner of the world.

CHAPTER 3

Memorial Day Parade and New Friendships

*A*nyone who knows me can tell you I like fire engines, steam engines and jet engines. I would love to own one of each, or at least I thought so in my early years. This find was one that I had been waiting for. When we went into the barn and I saw this bright red fire engine, my mind started whirling again; I wondered where they got it, how much they paid for it, and I wondered if they would sell it. I kept quiet as we walked around it. Mary, whose husband Dave was the owner, explained that much like myself, Dave had always wanted a shiny red fire truck, only he set out to get one.

I had read about this town and their annual Memorial Day celebration, which was one of the largest in Illinois. I saw the picture of Dave driving his fire truck at the front of the parade just like the newspaper article said he had done for the last 40 years. I had to find out about this when I read about it a few years ago and always wanted to find a reason to go. Since it was already summer, and I had already missed the Memorial Day parade, I made a google on the interwebs and in a few clicks, I found that someone named Bill Morrison had been in charge of this parade for the last 30 years. Bill was a fixture around town and it was not really hard to come up with an email address as contact information for him. After I introduced myself and explained my fire truck obsession via email, Bill replied quickly and seemed very friendly. He suggested that we set up a time to talk and I could call him when we could spend more time. With that we set a date for the next week and I anxiously looked forward to the call.

When the day arrived, Bill promptly answered the phone on the second ring and said that he had done some inquiries for me already. He invited me out for lunch where we could meet the owner and go on over to his farm and see the truck in person. That seemed like a good idea, so I told him that I would get back with him in the next couple of weeks.

As plans go, I had one and it seemed fine. No reason to rush it and so in the summer of 2011, I got tied up in another project and pushed this meeting off until the fall, which turned into winter which turned into spring. And here I was, like a school kid who had put off doing his assignments in a timely manner, I was now looking at another Memorial Day fast approaching. I had been keeping busy following other leads and family things, so I begged off one more time and told Bill I still wanted to do this lunch and meet him and Dave, but it was going to have to be put off a little longer. Bill was easy going and said no problem, anytime you want, just give me a call.

Well, I procrastinated for another year, and then another. You see, these stories don't really have any order of occurrence, just whenever

I get around to writing them after I outline the concept. Since I already had the bulk of the work finished, I saw no real problem until I called Bill once again in 2017. This time he told me that Dave had come down with some health issues the last year and he wasn't going to be able to drive in the parade that year, or probably any future parades either. I thought the absolute worst of myself at that time.

Bill said that we make plans, and God laughs. I said that since it was still early March, surely they could find someone to drive the fire engine in their parade. Bill said that there is quite a bit of preparation to get a 1948 Seagraves Fire Engine ready to roll and that, while Dave has no problem with designating a substitute driver, he needed someone mechanically inclined to get the truck ready. I suggested that maybe I could be of some assistance as I was a mechanic on both gasoline and diesel engines. I never worked on a fire engine, but since it wasn't needed to extinguish a burning house, maybe I could help. Bill thought about it and we agreed to meet the next morning for breakfast.

Bill, Dave and Mary had arrived early at the diner and were quite prepared with manuals and books and boxes of documents to show me. After a light breakfast and a heavy indoctrination as to what I was getting myself into, we agreed to go to their farm and see the actual piece of equipment.

On the ride out, I found out that Mary and Dave had gotten married at St. Sebastian Catholic church in 1967 in their small town of Dellshire in southern Illinois. They had both come from farm families and both of their parents had provided a small plot of ground for them to start out on their new and future life. They had their ups and downs, good times in bed and were blessed with many happy and healthy children.

As with farm life, they all participated and each helped the other. Family life on a farm can be a combination of things, much like in any family, however, the closeness of this life is what builds and molds each. The one thing about farm life however, is that the siblings all can count on one another. Just as with a team of horses pulling together, those in a farm family all pull together mostly because they can see from day to day the need to work and produce as a family and not as a group heading in different directions.

This farm was successful, raising beans and corn and thrived through the years. Buying a piece of land here and another over there, they were able to develop a nice farm of almost ten sections. The family knew that Dave loved fire engines and even spent time as a volunteer in the township fire department.

Sometime in 1977, they found a very used Seagraves fire engine for sale and after a little negotiation, brought it home on a flatbed provided by the seller. Dave was speechless when he saw it. He spent the next couple of years tinkering around with it and was finally asked to drive it in the annual 1981 Dellshire Memorial Day Parade.

Dave had been driving it in every Memorial Day Parade since. And now it was time to let someone else take over. About that time we pulled into their farm and up to the barn. We all got out and helped Dave into his wheelchair and followed him past the barn where he opened the doors to an outbuilding that held his prize trophy.

There it stood in its shiny beauty. A red pumper with the hoses still perfectly folded in the back. There was a white roof over the top with a shiny bright polished nickel siren on the nose of its hood. The hood was folded back on both sides showing the meticulously clean engine. I remarked how I had pretty much expected an oil sodden, beat up old relic, on its last legs……..Dave, said, no, that would be me.

We had a good laugh and were given the premiere tour of that machine. Why Fredric Seagrave himself could not have been prouder of this engine!

I climbed over and under that truck many times that day to get to see all of the adjustment checklist items that were nothing but essential to its proper and safe operation. Only when Dave was completely satisfied that everything had been checked and double checked, were we allowed to turn it over. It was like a symphony trying to tune up after not playing for a year. Very slowly at first, and there were some pops, wheezes and snaps, but they quickly quieted and soon the engine was humming like a well tuned orchestra. A smile of contentment was on Dave's face and Mary had a tear in her eye as she watched him.

I agreed to come back the next week after going over the books and manuals that, even though they came into the diner with them, all left with me. I was to study the manuals and be ready to do a 12 gallon oil change, a coolant change, a battery top off, fuel filters drain and change, and a hydraulic filter and oil change. Now I don't mind a little work now and then, but when I added up all of the fluids that I was to drain, flush and replace, I would be a walking toxic waste dump. Bill chided me about being a lazy city boy, but he said that he would help me haul the stuff in his truck and find a proper disposal place for all 40 plus gallons of it.

I became very good friends that spring with Dave and Bill with the work, searching for special filters and parts and just knocking around with a couple of very nice gentlemen who had also served our country back during the Vietnam war. They never talked much about it, but I could tell these were some special people. When Bill got out of school, he followed in his father's footsteps and became a carpenter, but he soon joined the service. He joined the Air Force reserves and was activated almost immediately. Over the the years Bill developed a strong attachment to his commitment and rose through the ranks until he finally retired with the rank of Chief Master Sergeant. This is no small accomplishment as The Chief Master Sergeant of the Air Force is a unique non-commissioned rank in the United States Air Force. The holder of this rank and position of office represents the highest enlisted level of leadership in the Air Force. He also used his GI Bill to finish college and get his teaching certificate, but he soon found himself with a growing family and the call back to his roots and continue with the family contracting business which is where you can find him anytime you go looking for him. Quite a unique man to be able to call my friend!

When the time came for the parade, I was well versed in the history of the parade and felt right in place when it started out that Memorial Day morning. Bill had driven the fire engine into its place at the front of the Parade with Dave riding shotgun, before any marching band, before any of the self-aggrandizing politicians and right behind the color guard, where both Bill and Dave stood to salute when it was finally positioned to start.

Then Bill motioned over to me to step up on the side board. He said that Dave wanted me to ride there and ring the bell. That parade was large, and it snaked through the town, past buildings new and old, past residential areas and business areas. If you drive through any small town, you may believe that they all look the same. Well, some of the features, buildings and infrastructure can be copied and with just a slight glance, you could make that mistake and place them all in the same bucket. BUT! You would be doing yourself a big dis-service. The uniqueness of each of the town squares, each of the city halls, as well as each and every building you see will guide you through a history with as much details as you want; It's all up to you. You can look at it and pass on, or, you can look at each and try to imagine it when it was built, the people who built it and their stories. You can think of each decade as it left it's marks, the weathers, the wars, the civil strife. Each of these issues all leave their marks. Its all up to you. I was very fortunate to have such keepers of the verbal history sitting with me point these things out and more. Now here we were packed with the many townsfolk who had come to watch this parade and its many floats, antique cars and trucks, of course the Shriners were there in full force with their large Harleys all the way down to their mini bikes and ATVs.

Every high school marching band from two counties was there and any citizen who just wanted to be in a parade was there proudly waving the American flag with a smile that would take a week to wipe off.

And did you know that if you own a convertible in a small town, you are almost at celebrity status? Everyone wants you in every parade! So maybe I don't need a fire truck to be in a parade....

And so it was that I participated in one of the longest continuously occurring Memorial Day Parades in America, with my two newest friends, Bill and Dave.

I am looking forward to next year's parade.

CHAPTER 4

The Scotty, the VW and the Hippie

*T*he diner we stopped at this afternoon was off the beaten path in Waverley, Illinois and although we were only about 50 miles from our home, and probably averaging only 30 miles per hour, we had clocked over 120 miles on the car today. With the aid of Google Maps aerial view we were able to investigate quite a few places that may have hidden some interesting barns. We were starting to go "snow blind" as everything about these barns was beginning to look the same. Time for a late lunch. We found a nice place right downtown and of course found a parking space right in front.

Pat ordered the cheeseburger with fries and I had a couple of side orders: buffalo hot wings, onion rings and a salad. As we were discussing our notes during the serving of the meals, the waitress overheard us. There were a few other tables in the diner on this late Tuesday afternoon but none seemed rushed, so we included her in our discussion. After telling her about our "Barn Stories" project, she seemed interested and then walked back to the kitchen after topping off a few coffee cups. We could hear her speaking to the cook about something. We continued with our meal and observed the others sharing the room and time with us. Every now and then the little bell above the door would announce another hungry mouth or two, each being greeted or acknowledged by at least one other inhabitant of the establishment. It seemed that there was only one waitress and the cook in this place and even though the tables were almost at capacity, this place was running very smoothly. It was a nice place to spend some time. There was a shelf running along the top of the front windows which continued down each wall about two feet shy of the ceiling and maybe about 7 feet off the floor. Just enough to keep curious hands from examining one of the many items of that collection of circus memorabilia that were up there. Mostly ceramic animals, circus cars, trucks, trains, tents, and whatever other carnival paraphernalia the owners had collected over the years. "Hey Rube!"* was a strange name for a diner and exactly why we had walked into this joint.

Note: *"Hey Rube" was a call initiated by a carney calling for all workers (carneys) to drop whatever they were doing and come running to aid their cohorts in whatever disagreement, confrontation or fist fight they might be needed in.

After our waitress, Bonnie had made her rounds once again, I let her know we were ready for our check. I raised my hand and rubbed my thumb and fingers together, she acknowledged me by nodding and disappearing into the kitchen again. She walked back out writing on her pad and when she got to our table, she handed me a note with a name and address on it. I also noticed the cook followed her from the kitchen. He was standing next to her while she explained that this farm was a little down the road and that she had already spoken to the owners and told them we would be stopping by.

The cook, Frank, who had his name tattooed on his bicep, jumped in; Sara and her husband "Tulie" Thomas had a farm down the road. "We only see Tulie and that car every couple of years, but it's him every time. You can't miss him" he said. "Miss what?" I asked. "The hippie VW," he said. It's the only one around here and it's been around here for, and he looked at Bonnie; "30? 40 Years?" Someone at the next table said, no, it's more like 60 years. Our heads spun as someone behind us joined in and said "It's a 1958! Do the Math! 61 years!" And just like that I was introduced to Steve Reynolds, the high school math teacher. Khaki pants, brown hushpuppies and a brown sweater vest with a white shirt with the top buttoned. Honest to god he had a pocket protector AND a slide-rule attached to his belt!!!

He sure wouldn't fool anyone on "Whats's my line?"

Ok, so I gotta ask him: What's with dressing like this? I mean NOBODY uses a slide rule anymore. It was at this point I felt Pat kicking under the table and as I looked around, I saw that just about everybody seemed to have just stepped out of the late 50's or early 60's. One by one they told me that once a year everybody dresses up like THEY thought they did as Seniors in their old high schools.

Ok, our interest was piqued and soon a sketchy story was taking place. All the while more and more people were pulling up chairs to join in adding to the chaos, er, story. Pat was taking notes while I would try and slow the story enough that we could keep somewhat accurate details.

There was a tale there and after about 2 hours, well through the dinner rush hour, we flushed out what we thought might be a memorable trip to the new farm. Bonnie assured us that the Thomas

Farm would welcome us tomorrow morning around 9 AM if we would like the opportunity. We agreed and were then directed down the road to another motel for the evening. What a joint this one was, all knotty pine paneling in the place with two twin beds. Each bed had a coin acceptor that when activated would shake and rattle the bed and make so much racket that EVERYONE in the place knew that you plopped in 25 cents for the experience. But ONLY once. I don't know if anyone ever used those things, but they certainly gave you the ride of your life if you tried to ride one out. I couldn't imagine ANYone, going anymore than one round. Which by the way was 15 minutes.

The next morning, we tried the advertised, complimentary "executive" breakfast at the motel. Stale bagels, toast and jam. I didn't bother looking for any executives.

9 AM and this beautiful spring morning offered the hope of a great start! Once the breakfast digested......

We found the Thomas Farm just as described by Bonnie, Frank, Steve and the others. It was a working farm with all the sights, sounds and smells accompanying it.

Mr. and Mrs. Thomas greeted us at the door. After pleasantries were exchanged she invited us into the "parlor" where we were seated and offered coffee and some fresh baked pastries. This was a typical farmhouse, with clapboard siding and ornamental woodwork, both inside and out. Well maintained. I was told this was the second house on the property as the original had burned down in the early 1940's. The Thomas's, Sara and Tulie, were married in the late 1940's.

Tulie's brother and wife, Sam and Lisa Thomas ran the local dry goods store in town after deciding that they were more cut out to be merchants than farmers. It seemed to be much easier to decide what items the town might need than to try and figure out seed yield or the weather. Yes, this was a bit before Dollar General had a store on every entry to each town. Stocking belts, socks, underwear, and coats was easy. In the midwest you know two things for certain; It's going to get cold in the winter and it's going to get hot in the summer time. Throw in some fashionable clothing in between and they had it made; or so they thought. They had a daughter, Jennifer who was born in 1950 and was raised by her parents with lots of visits to the farm in her younger days. There was some falling out between the daughter and her parents early on, but Jennifer remained very close with her Aunt Sara and Uncle Tulie.

Through high school Jennifer would live on the farm off and on as life with a teenager in the 60's was strenuous for her parents. Jennifer was becoming very independent and the development of the hippie movement pushed her away from her parents' very conservative life. Tulie and Sara became partners in Jennifer's life and try as they might, they could not mend the growing chasm between the rebellious teenager and her parents. As an only child and being a girl AND growing up in the 50's was tough on her. She had a few friends, and one or two very close to her over the years, but as life goes on, friends would come and go. Jennifer often relied on her aunt to confide in and sometimes Tulie as well.

Life on the farm also presented problems, the biggest was her need for transportation from the farm to school and her friends. Tulie bought her an older VW to help. This proved to be seen as *interfering* with the parents notion of trying to do their duty of raising Jennifer and caused an even greater chasm between them. Both parents and aunt and uncle only wanted what would be best for her, they agreed on that. Many times Tulie would come in from the field in the evening to find Sara and Jennifer engrossed in some "urgent" girl time issues that he couldn't understand, nor wanted to anyway.

One day Tulie found Jennie and her friends from school decorating her car with little personal touches, the biggest of which was their decision to paint the car with any number of colorful flowers and splashes of neon colors. A regular flower mobile as they called it. It was the only one like it anyone had seen in these parts. As you might imagine, it was taken as an affront to the conservative community, a symbol of rebellion to the more liberal of them and just "a puzzlement" to Tulie who loved taking them both to see the movie versions of actual broadway shows on occasion in the local theatre. Tulie may have just remembered Yule Brenner in "The King and I" at one theater. I didn't ask.

"Would you like to see it?"

"Of course!" We were anxious with anticipation when we were escorted to the barn. As usual, some equipment had to be moved, but we could almost feel the radiant paint burning though the tarp covering the vehicle.

When Tulie pulled the tarp back, with our gentle help of course, we were immediately transported back to the late 1960's in the Haight Ashbury district of San Francisco! Young people crowding the sidewalks of "the Haight", each one wearing bellbottom jeans,

Chambray shirts and TIE DYED EVERYTHING! Any type of hat was cool if you had the confidence and most that made the trip to San Fransisco did! Wine, and pot was in the air everywhere. The shops in the district were attuned to this new group and they welcomed the newly formed "hippies" as a new adventure waiting to occur.

Well getting back to Waverly, I mean this car was magical! Both Pat and I were astonished at the detail that was there for such an old car. It was dripping with memories. Although Pat and I had really not participated in the hippie movement from our lot in life, we had brushed up against it easily during our high school days. Pat's days at Rosati Kain High School in St. Louis between 1967 through 1971 had her involved in painting, writing and singing as well as lots of other projects evolving from a Catholic, all girls, city high school. When we met in 1971 during college at St. Louis University, one of my friends from pre-med was copying her chemistry notes. He went on to become a doctor. I did not, but she married me, so, looks like I won!

We looked the car over, keenly aware of the hand-painted details from decades ago. Large flowers, small flowers, leaves, vines, A few bumble bees, and a Scottish Terrier?
Sara explained that the Scottie was the mascot of the Waverly schools. I can only imagine the PTA meeting when *that* decision was finally made. Terriers are sometimes mean, of course stubborn, and tenacious at best....but they certainly would not NOT instill FEAR into another high school opponent vying for Homecoming honors! I can just imagine the soccer mom standing there insisting that these fierce Waverly Warriors be known as the Waverly Scotties! No use dwelling on that anyway, THAT ship had sailed.

Sara went on to tell me how much music meant to Jennie at that time. Her favorite songs, her favorite bands. At this time, you may want to put on a few tunes from that era. Never mind! I just decided to add a Musical appendix to this book so that you can listen to the music as you are reading it. Lets see if it works? Jefferson Airplane and Grace Slick were the musical gods that they worshiped along with Jim Morrison and the Doors, Donovan, Rotary Connections. If this were an e-book, I would have the music playing already; As a matter of fact, I will include a digital play list in the back of this book so that you may enjoy this music as I am while I am writing about it! Many of the bands and many of the songs were still fresh in our minds, being from that era.

Jennie had a boyfriend at that time. Jake was what they remembered. He was a high school "jock" who excelled at sports, especially football. Friday night football in southern Illinois was then, and still is today, an institution not to be mocked, nor taken for granted.

Entering the gymnasium through its main doors, was the lobby with the large hallway to the left would lead to the girls locker rooms and the hallway to the right would lead to the boys locker rooms which would then both empty its athletes out onto the gym floor. But standing in the lobby of this or any high school gymnasium, you will see the inevitable trophy case. How much emotion is there to imagine when you look at whatever year's State Championship Trophy, with the accompanying team photo. The players, the athletes, the cheerleaders, the band members, the pom pom squad. Each one of these persons have left a bit of themselves right here for you to see and perhaps, even share some of those emotions. Try it sometime. Even though I was not much of an athlete in school, I was the school photographer, and so, yes, even a bit of emotion was there for me to share as well.

Tulie said that you could still see Jake's trophies as well as the State Championship Trophy that they brought home that senior year enshrined for eternity in the school's trophy case.

It was always assumed that the two of them would go to college. Jake would stay close to home and apply to SIU at Carbondale to study engineering while Jennie, who applied to many schools, and was accepted at all of them, decided on Carnegie-Mellon University on a music scholarship. Her instrument of choice was flute, but she enjoyed picking mandolin in some of the local bluegrass bands around town while growing up. Sara pointed out the second Scotty pictured on the car above the left rear fender. "Guess what the Carnegie-Mellon mascot is," she asked, quickly followed by a very distinct eyebrow raise......."Think it's a coincidence?"

Times being what they were, the military draft had initiated a birthday lottery and Jake's birthday turned up as number 94. It was just assumed that anything below 100 was going to 'Nam, and Jake did. No student deferment. Pack your bag and get to the selective service office in the Federal Building in Benton Illinois. Jake passed his physical with no problems and was sent to boot camp in the middle of Missouri, Fort Leonard Wood, or as the inhabitants called it "Fort lost in the woods".

Many letters were sent forth and back between the two and, as they both realized that they had a duty to family and our country, they accepted their fates as two people in love do. Jennie and Jake found a few times to meet as she could drive her VW to camp when she came home from school and have a motel room right outside the base. Although this was *not* the Taj Mahal by any stretch of the imagination, they made do. However, there was one hotel, that they decided NOT to stay in as Jenn confided in Sara once. It was getting late and they just gave in and against their better judgement, they stopped and after retrieving their keys from an Indian man seated behind 2 inches of bullet proof glass they walked down the side and passed each and every occupied room. As they unlocked the door and looked into a bed with just one dirty sheet on it with a single, red, lightbulb that at least LIT when Jake flipped the switch. When their eyes adjusted to the filmy red light that the bulb shone on everything, there they saw it. A sign hanging just above the opening to the bathroom where a door should be. The sign said " Please do not Clean Game in Room". They found another hotel about 3 hours down the road where they had a hot shower and a good laugh.

In an unusual turn of events, Jake was promoted to Pfc. and then to corporal. He was asked to stay on as an instructor for an indefinite amount of time, which he eagerly accepted. Time was moving on and Jennie's trips back home became shorter and fewer. Jake was shipped out the next summer and sent to Vietnam. He spent six months "in country". The letters change as she felt him drifting away from the boy she knew in school to someone she hardly recognized. How she wanted to go over there and tell them to give her back the young innocent boy that she loved. She began to dread each letter she received as they only depressed her.

August 1971 she received a call from Jake's parents. He had died in a fire fight the week before. His remains were being sent back home. She did not attend the funeral.

Jennie packed up his remembrances and hers from the farm, put them in the VW and left it parked in the barn, dropped out of school and found her way to San Francisco on a Greyhound bus. She didn't want to drive out herself and just wanted the time alone on the bus. So one variation of the story was that she took the Greyhound first to Vancouver BC, over to Calgary, then Winnipeg and finally to Salt Lake City and then down to San Fransisco. They think that she was on a bus for over a month during this time trying to decide how to sort out her life.

Her letters back home became fewer and fewer, but Sara and Tulie read each one of them out loud whenever they received one. Eventually she would describe the fun she had found in her new life. Once she settled down into her apartment she started to meld into the person that she had been searching for in her teens. One of the letters asked how her car was. They realized it had been sitting in the barn for a couple of years without even having been started. Tulie decided to pull the battery and put it up on blocks with the anticipation that he would get it primed and ready for her when next she came home.

By this time, Jennie had been living life as if she had been born to be a hippie queen. She had found a small apartment with two others in the 'Haight". She landed a job teaching music and as a counter person at "The Musical Apothecary", a local music store, where she made quite a few friends and met some phenomenal musicians. Jerry Garcia had once come in and purchased some strings from her and he invited her out to hear his band at a local park. When she arrived and he saw her in her long, flowing, flowered dress with her hair cascading over her shoulders, he immediately asked if she would like to come up on stage with him to inspire him. She did, and found that it was a wonderful way to spend the afternoon, spinning and dancing and "floating above the clouds". I'm sure there were some herbs passed around and smoked. She never admitted this in her letters to Sara, but when she phoned and spoke to Tulie, she hinted at it. She also understood now, that funny smell that was always coming from the bags in the barn loft. They were there sometime and then they would just be gone. She really hadn't smoked in high school and she and Jake stayed away from those who did.

So now, she was starting to understand the spartan, nondescript lifestyle that her Aunt and Uncle had lived. And why her very strict and conservative parents did not approve of them either. Tulie and Sara did not socialize much. There were times that groups of people would show up late at night at the barn with a truck and load something (those burlap sacks) into the back of the truck. And then the arguments that her parents would always have with her Aunt and Uncle. And finally, the fact that Tulie always had time and money for her. Why even when she was in school, Tulie paid for her apartment off campus, and her allowance now that she was in California. She realized that she could never make it in California if she were to rely on her own finances, but she never really pondered that too much.

She traveled around California to visit music festivals all the time. Her part-time job at the music store in "the Haight" was always waiting for her. She even got to play mandolin on stage with Jerry Garcia and his collection called the Grateful Dead. To this day Tulie argues that Workingman's Dead is their quintessential album. For whatever that is worth. On one of the many music stages, she met Jerry Rubin and Abby Hoffman as a side note into her life.

She was still working at the music store when a very straight looking young man came in to buy some nylon strings for his guitar. She noticed his wavy blond hair and broad smile that "melted her heart instantly". He noticed that she short changed him 10 dollars on that transaction. When his smile still stayed as he pointed out the mistake, she immediately apologized, turned beet red and made two more mistakes making the change until, with his help, and strong hands they got it straightened out.

Randy, or Rand, as he preferred to be called, was part of the establishment who worked in the downtown skyscrapers. He liked the music here and would be seen at many of the street festivals every weekend. He also stopped in the Musical Apothecary every visit to purchase a new set of strings almost every week. Jennie figured Rand to be an audiophile as he assured her that he would wear out a set of strings and that he could tell the difference. She didn't care, she liked the attention. As time drew on Jennie and Rand became quite good friends, but nothing romantic ever developed between them.

She took trips back home to visit the family every year, and every year Tulie would work on the car to make sure it was just perfect for her to drive. Then he would button it back up again until the next visit. Eventually the trips back were every two years, then three, then five, and then only on that rare occasion that someone had died, or a wedding. A holiday family gathering was no guarantee that she would be back. Tulie, however, would religiously work on the car and get it in shape for Road America, as if that mattered. He was happy for this time to work in solitude with his memories.

Tulie and Sara both wiped their eyes at the end of this story signaling that Jennie no longer returns, but promises to with each letter. She is still single. The Musical Apothecary has long closed and she is making ends meet working as an office manager at a local stock exchange downtown.

Oh, and she moved to Oakland. She has a Scottish terrier who sits for hours watching her and wondering what she will do next. She still loves music and has been following The Tower Of Power for the last 40 or so years. Tulie likes the music.

CHAPTER 5

Poverty, Pride and Perseverance

*D*uring the drive our eyes would often catch a glimpse of some tell-tale item that would pique our interest. We would pull in, ask some questions, and either get run off or invited in. Sometimes when we got invited in we would feel it's time to "r-u-n-n-o-f-t" (if you've ever watched "Oh Brother Where Art Thou"). At any rate, today found us driving very slowly down an old gravel road, through a creek and finally into the "actual farm compound".

On this one it would be called a housebarn. This was a combination that was brought over from Scandinavia at the turn of the last century. Instead of the barn being a separate building, the house and barn were connected together. This makes plenty of sense in the high northern climates of Finland, Norway or Sweden, but during the warm southern months around the midwestern USA, it made for some peculiar odors in the house.

This place was built many, many years ago and although it may have been the pride of a few generations, it has finally fallen into great disarray. As we pulled in we became acutely aware of our surroundings and questioned whether or not we should really proceed. Well, we were already here and I could now see a large, solitary figure walking up to the car. He got to us rather quickly and before I could open the door to get out, he pressed it back closed, leaned on it with his hands through the open window, his palms pressing down as if to show his ability to move this car if he had to. "May I help you?", he asked in a pleasant voice.

"Good Morning." I said.
He looked around and replied; "Yes, it is a mighty fine morning at that," and he leaned back down with his head almost inside the window now.

Again, he asked politely: "May I help you?"

I introduced us both as Pat got out of the car on the side not pinned back. This, I could tell, made the big man uncomfortable, as he stood up to watch her while still keeping one hand on my door. I cleared my throat to get his attention and explained that we were just driving and saw his interesting "housebarn" and told him that we have never seen one of these this far south in the USA before. THAT got his attention.

He pulled back from the door and looked at the building, much like, I would imagine, the original owners did so many times when it was new. He had a smile, small, but you could tell a smile just the same. I took the cue and got out to admire the structure with him. "These are interesting lines here," I pointed out how the steep roofs were not only good to keep the snow load off, but for ventilation both in the summer and winter. I asked if there were any drop down panels in the house to deflect the rising heat back downstairs for the changing seasons. Well, that just opened the floodgates. Soon Pat and I were learning the entire history of the house. Before I could stop him to explain our project, he had given us a synopsis of the 150 year history of that "housebarn".

Josh and Donna Ebermann are the current owners' names. Donna had come out to see what was going on, and, after a suitable amount of time to size up and assess the situation, she had come to the same conclusion as Josh. We were harmless.

It was a brisk winter day this morning, and everyone was wearing winter gear, Pat and I in our red and green Eddie Bauer jackets, and Josh and Donna in their well worked and worn Carharts. We were invited into the barn where I immediately saw the remains of some old car or truck. Just the chassis was there with either flat or deflated tires on every corner. There was a dented and somewhat twisted black and gold two tone fender leaning against the wall. There were also plenty of farm implements and tools as well as lots of boxes, bags and piles of "stuff" you just can't get rid of because you might need it someday. I asked about the car frame and that question was quickly brushed aside. They started asking me about the book we were researching for, and our more specific answers caused them to look at each other and whisper.

We were now getting the "bum's rush" out of here right now! As we were standing by our car with the doors being held open by both Josh and Donna, we said our sterile goodbyes with as much emotion as would be allowed at the time.

"Well, that went well, didn't it?", observed Pat as more of an accusation than a question.

We drove in silence for a while, each re-creating the encounter in our minds to figure out what may have triggered our abrupt send-off. It was not unlike "the great skedaddle", we northerners have faced from our southern brothers over the years. We stopped at a roadside bar and grill for an early lunch and a beer. Unfortunately they didn't serve beer until after lunch for some reason, so we just had a couple of burgers at the bar. There were a few locals wandering in for lunch as we enjoyed our cheeseburgers, however, we noticed that most came in well after noon and ordered a beer right up. The bartender saw us eyeing him opening six or seven bottles for one group and nonchalantly set two in front of us. "First one is on the house"; he said. We didn't even pretend to understand the logic here so we just enjoyed the beer. It was warm inside and we didn't have anywhere else to go so we had another beer. As some of the lunch crowd had headed back off to work (I assume) I bought a round for the house, $12 including tip. Pat said "big spender", but soon the thanks were coming in and one by one the locals would come over to thank and shake my hand.

After the next round, I asked about the Ebermann Farm down the road. With as much of a skeptical eye as Josh and Donna had, we soon saw the same thing from this group. They weren't much help either. How do you know them? Where are you from? Why do you want to know? Geez, it was almost like I was back at the Ebermann Farm. We explained that we were writing a book about interesting things we saw or heard about in barns around the state as we were driving. I had a choice to make: pay the tab and get out of "Dodge" or buy another round and see if I could break through the ice. This was shaping up to be another "discretion is the better part of valor," so I agreed with her.

I offered up another round as Pat shook her head and disappeared out the door.

Everyone was now sitting at the bar as the lunch crowd had abandoned the tables for either work or to continue what might turn out to be an interesting afternoon at the bar. If it didn't, who cares, not a problem either way.

After the customary round was distributed, a complimentary shake and roll of the dice by Larry at the end of the bar showed his ivory poker hand had beaten the bartender, Greg. Larry ordered a round for the house which resulted in a shot glass placed upside down in front of each person since they already had a beer. This is a normal custom in the USA that I have traveled, but not so much in the rest of the world. My travels have taken my son and me to Australia where we saw the Southern Cross but I will be darned if I can remember anything like this in the Land Down Under.

This place had an old Wurlitzer Jukebox with the colorful lights and bubbles flowing up each side of it until they curved into a sacred arch that most of us drunks recognize, not from a church entrance, but this magic sound machine. Ever notice how the jukebox makes your favorite song sound better than it ever has in your car or your home radio? Well it does.

I asked Greg for some change for a 5 dollar bill for the jukebox. He reached into a bag behind the counter and gave me a handful of quarters all painted red. I had forgotten about the "bar"quarters. They were the bait that the bartender used to start the jukebox playing. When the jukebox mechanic from the vending machine company that owned the machine would come around to collect the money every week, the red quarters would always be returned to the bar as seed money to be recycled again each night.

I walked over to the jukebox and started reading the selections. Johnny Cash, Merle Haggard, Willie Nelson, and Patsy Cline favorites were in the first row of handwritten titles and artists. You know, faded white paper tabs with the song title of the "A" side written on the top line, the "B" side written on the bottom and the artist name in the middle separated by red lines.

The next row were the more contemporary or modern Country artists with their hits, followed by a couple of rows of AC/DC, Foreigner, RUSH, Bob Seeger and of course the BOSS, Bruce Springstein. You know it's a REAL hangout when you find "Happy Birthday" and the "Anniversary Waltz".

I had been around these joints all of my life. I was about to tame the crowd. You see, if you go over to the end of the list, you will usually find at least a few blank selections. Here is the secret: the locals all have their favorite songs on those blanks. It's really quite an honor in some parts of the country. Now there are probably some graphic lyrics too. Way before WAP and NWA came out, there were recordings that were adults-only. The Rodeo Song is my favorite of these and most every honky-tonk in the land has it hidden on one of the last selections. Thanks to my good friend Curt who clued me in to that handy piece of information.

I plunked a handful of quarters into every blank selection that was there. Pretty soon the entire bar of drunks was amazed at my magical choice of music for the afternoon. We were drinking and cursing and throwing popcorn like a bunch of kids when Pat came back about 4:30. She had driven down the road and secured a room for the night because she knows me so well. I'm not sure how long we've been married, but we ARE on our second bottle of tabasco sauce!

So now, Pat asked about the Ebermann Farm and the stories couldn't come fast enough. We drank, had dinner, watched the dinner rush come and the dinner rush go, and drank some more, all the time collecting research on the farm and what stories it might hold.

I woke up in the Friendly Acres Motel Guest Suite #7, and I think we were the only ones in the whole motel. We had collected a lot of stories and Pat had spent the morning sorting through her notes while I spent the morning, well, I had been drinking all day and night...... We had enough details to sort of figure out what was happening here. I thought that we could break through and get Josh and Donna to agree to let us in, so to speak.

The Ebermanns were an isolated couple even though the family name was one of the older ones in the community. They had some history that they were not proud of and through no fault of their own, had felt, well, embarrassed or ashamed were probably too strong of words to describe it, but they did not feel 'accepted' by their neighbors...... for decades! As far as we could figure, poverty, hard times, recession, are all words that were no strangers to this family. The group at the bar last night led us to this conclusion, with a collection of "Cat", John Deere, Peterbilt, Frieghtliner hats and even a Volvo thrown in to balance things out. For one thing, we notice the make up of the crowd before we even start to think about pulling any of my usual tricks in these bars. We seemed to be in pretty good company. Poverty plays no favorites and the community was well represented here with a reasonable amount of Blacks, Hispanics and Asians dispersed through most of these joints that we had found ourselves in. Don't get me wrong, you can just as easily find a racist bar with the "Stars and Bars" proudly honored behind some bars, but for my freedoms in this Grand Old Country, I always choose to find a historically and racially mixed crowd for my comfort level. Its keep most of the teeth in my head from being loosened and my eyes from being blacked. I've had my bad days and nights. So I learn when to keep my mouth shut and when to seek the safety of another harbor as we move along.

After going through our notes that morning, we believed that there was no real reason for them to be ostracized. If they felt that way, it was the Ebermanns' perception. Not at all what we could extract from the movers and shakers of this community even with the small sample size represented in the group of drunks we quizzed yesterday.

From what we could determine, the Ebermann name had appeared on the tax rolls around the 1920's when Wayne and Edna Ebermann bought a farm described by two very long paragraphs of "Beginning from the cornerstone on the Northwest corner of City Hall, continue in a northerly direction 2500 feet until........"you get the idea. Suffice it to say that it described the property where we had met Josh and Donna. The local lore was that the farm had produced more than a couple of good crops of corn before the Depression hit.

As everyone back then, they needed to make ends meet and began selling some of their corn to a moonshiner across the Wabash in Indiana. Then at some point, Wayne tried his hand at making moonshine for a while. Apparently he was doing well and there were some rumors that he was supplying Al Capone in Chicago, but no real proof would be found to tie them together.

Sometime in the late 50's Wayne was caught and spent five years in Statesville. When he got out in the early 60's he was much more careful and secretive about his work.

Running moonshine in an old "tanker" as the cars had become to be known also allowed one to really take in the beauty of this Shawnee Nation Forest that the National Parks Service oversees. Rim Rock trail has such a beauty to it in any season but if you really want to see it in all of it's glory, come on out here during the changing of the seasons from fall to winter just before the trees drop their foliage. There leaves and vines paint this area with such a palate of colors that would make most any artist just stare in awe before giving up and leaving the masters alone with their work.

Wayne had always liked big and fast cars and as soon as his son Josh could drive, he had him running moonshine up and down the state with him to learn the ropes. One of the locals last night told a drunken story that his father had told him about a 1956 Ford Fairlane with the largest engine that could be had in one. Unlike all other moonshine tankers, this one was flashy and attracted a lot of attention. Wayne had every option that would make it run faster and lost every option that just made weight. It was seen around the area quite often, you could NEVER, NOT notice it.

After Wayne passed, Josh settled down and helped his mother run what was left of the business. He got married sometime in the late

1960's to Donna Jo Fields. The feds were tying up some old open case files and decided to press Josh for some RICO charge based on a traffic ticket he got while driving back from a "blind drop". Even though he was empty, there was some loose end that Josh agreed to plead to if that would keep his 68 year old mother out of jail, as that was the bait in the trap. When Josh returned to the farm, he and Donna tried as they could to work it, but hard times, pride and reputations seemed to hold them down. They eventually wound up leasing out some of the property and sharecropped the rest. They tried a roadside stand finally just to keep a little income so they could pay taxes.

Back when times were good Wayne had the foresight to pay off the mortgage, however the State of Illinois is hell on taxes and the Ebermanns always seemed to be far enough behind for the tax man to come knocking with his liens.

At least a phone call was in order. No one at the bar last night knew if they had a cell or a landline, nor could anyone recall if they currently even had a phone. Hanging around a little bar that could be found closest to the local jail would usually afford us a few people who would talk a little once they felt there was no harm in it. That and a few extra shot glasses backed up on the bar behind a talker's current beer. Seems Stag is the favorite beer around her. Even being that close to the Augie Busch headquarters about 300 miles northwest of this point.

We did a little PI work on our own, and found an old hand-printed ad tacked on the bulletin board in the local grocery. We had done our share of detective work in the past and knew some of the angles to work. Although we were not in need of "all types of junk hauled away", we copied the number that specified Ebermann Hauling.

I called it at last in the afternoon when I was feeling a bit better and had time to think this plan through. I was at least semi-cognizant when Donna answered the phone. I immediately identified myself and waited to see if she would reply or just hang up. When she asked what she could do for me, I found the entry that I was looking for. I explained that Pat and I felt bad about leaving them the way we did and would like to try and explain our project over a nice dinner that evening in the restaurant at the Historic Rose Hotel in Elizabethtown. I said: "Our treat" , and she said that she would speak to Josh and let us know. I offered my number but before I finished, she said, "It's on the cell."

The call came back almost before I put my phone back in my pocket. I recognized the number since I had just dialed it and answered; "Hello Donna" and was immediately interrupted as Josh identified himself. He started to explain that there was no need for a meal and that everything was left fine with them. I was insistent and finally he agreed to meet us in the dining room at 7PM Maybe it's just me but I could "feel" Donna glaring at him all the time he was saying "it's not necessary" until he finally gave in.

Pat went through our notes once more, calling out the highlights of points I may have missed or forgotten in a drunken fog the night before. I was looking through the interwebs for any information I could find about a 1956 Ford Fairlane with the specs that may or may not have been correct. One thing that was correct and everyone insisted upon the night before was that this car was very special, as only one had been made with the treasured "F" code high performance 300 hp engine.

Armed with what we thought was good intelligence, we met them at the agreed-upon time. I thought that Josh and Donna would feel more at ease in this neutral ground and that must have been what convinced them. Pleasantries were made and hands were shaken and smiles were exchanged.

Wow, I might have really blown this because when we finally arrived and started to walk in, Pat tugged my shirt and pointed to a sign announcing that just next door was the Hardin County Probation Office. Well, whatever it was, we were there and having a nice dinner just getting to know one another. One order of business during the meal was a toast to them and their future. They were impressed that Pat and I had known each other for over 50 years and had been married coming up on our 50th. We toasted with beer all around and as the evening went on, we developed an insight into the Ebermann family.

They indeed were a strong and proud family. Life had been hard on them, and they didn't resent anyone for their predicament. They accepted their "lot in life" with dignity although they would rather not socialize with anyone as they sincerely thought they were unworthy of any friendship. Their view of moonshine and bootlegging was very dark and conservative. Not only did they get what they deserved for being on the wrong side of the law, the prison sentences were looked upon by them as not a debt to society paid, but as a scarlet letter that identified them for all time as sinners in the eyes of God and the honorable citizens of this fine county.

Pat and I could only listen to their story which verified (mostly) the drunken tales we had heard the night before. By the end of the evening we had heard and understood these two souls, "working hard everyday to do their best for just one more day". Thank you to the team of Rodgers and Hammerstein for this quote again from the King and I.

After 3 hours, we decided to call it a night. As I paid the check, Josh insisted that I allow him to pick up the tip. When I did, he pulled out of his pocket a wadded up handful of singles and a couple of fives. When he began to count it out, I just accepted it and said, it was just fine.

We walked to the lobby and I asked if we could stop by in the morning so he could tell me a little bit more about the car in the barn. He smiled and said, "yeah, that's right, "Barn Stories". We agreed to return to their "housebarn" about 9 AM.

I had an idea. In talking to the two of them, they never centered any of their story around that car, the 1956 Ford, but they did acknowledge its existence and did not shy away from any details about it nor its blue ribbon birthright.

I did some more research on that car and found that it was indeed noticed as a Moonshine Runner at the dealership when Wayne had bought it. Its legacy was investigated sometime in the last century by some hot rod clubs who were interested in it. And one other thing.......Pat was flashing the lights on and off telling me that she had already checked out and we had to start moving:

Fade to flashback:"OK, OK! Let's just get going"...seems there was a Masseratti in the parking lot and she was looking at it.......I remember a car alarm in the background. Her curiosity got the best of her again. Just like 40 years ago. On one of our business trips Pat accompanied me and we were in Fort Lauderdale Florida for a week or so. Having a lot of family (on her side) we always had built in baby sitters. Plus, our home in the bluffs of the Mississippi was a great visit for a few days. So as I remember we had found a really cool, old school, Miami style nightclub. Dark interior, with little round tables with colored Hurricane lamps. These tables were just big enough to hold maybe 2 drinks. And offered a "Rat Pack" style of musical acts! We closed this one down and headed back to our beach front hotel, The Ocean Hacienda. It was 5 stories tall and we always go for the highest floor, so the trudge up 5 flights was in front of me as I looked up and immediately was jolted back to reality when a really LOUD car alarm went off from what I could tell was a CLASSIC Maserati, along with a accompanied siren and flashing lights. Just about then Pat came walking briskly past me and said, "come on, hurry up, we gotta get out of here."We were young, and we made it to the top of the stairs and into our room and, leaving the lights out, went out to our balcony to survey the "lay of the land" so to speak. There were police from every municipality, county and state highway patrol within a couple of minutes. Whoever owned this car was pretty well connected. He appeared in the parking lot in a robe and a young blond wandering along wearing a very sheer robe. Made me wish I had maybe stayed…..never mind. The hotel manager was there, and I could tell the owner did NOT want anything to do with the cops. Things died down within 15 minutes as we watched and toasted the last car to leave, Dade County Police. Did I mention that along with me being nosey, Pat has never exercised ANY bit of restraint in her curiosity on the classic automotive front when there was a convertible with the top down.? By the way, she had one too.

We made it to the farm on time and since no one was hung over, greeted each other like old family, long lost and finally reunited. No kidding! I mean, you would've thought Pat and Donna were going to bring out pictures of the last time we got together!

I was anxious to get to the barn but I didn't press it. Josh finally pointed to the barn doors which were both open and lighting up the interior like a chapel. I was again struck by the phenomenal workmanship and architecture of that building. Josh had pulled the parts and pieces of the Ford together into some semblance of a do-it-yourself full-sized car kit. He had even managed to get the rare "F" code engine and transmission hanging by a chain from the tractor backhoe attachment.

The fenders, trunk, and hood from what I could tell were all there….. just no body. We started looking at it and I could see that it was still the original black and gold, but with lots of oxidation. There were a couple of dents and some attempts at Bondo and body work that were never completed. You see, although Donna had instructions to keep the car hidden in the barn, she also had her brother, the mechanic, come over through those long years of Josh's incarceration and take the entire car apart. She had hoped that there would be no thought of "running liqueur" ever again. Josh must have agreed as that is the way that it had remained for the last several decades.

When I asked Donna if she thought her brother might help with a reconstruction project of the car, if of course they ever wanted to put it back together, I found that he had passed a few years back. She then told me that her brother was a mechanic at a local coal mine in the area back then. He had died of a common ailment among Illinois miners; black lung. A horrible disease that is caused by very small particles of coal dust that are inhaled while working underground in those cramped and less than well ventilated passages. While it is well known what causes it, it still occurs to this day as long as men have to take that work to provide for their family. Don't get me wrong, it is good paying work, however, there usually is just one ending for a miner who chooses this particular career.

"Well," I said, "do you know anything more about this car that you have here?" I felt like the guy on "Antique Roadshow". Both just looked at each other and shook their heads as they said "No." in unison.

Well, if you had a complete car, one like this from 1957 just sold last year at a well known automotive auction house for almost $225,000.00.

Their mouths fell open.

It was silent for quite some while.

When it finally soaked in, both Josh and Donna quickly hurried and pulled open another door in the barn and exposed the complete body. I checked the VIN, which was still intact and there was the "F"code signifying the holy grail! Then he motioned me inside and opened the glove box and pointed to the door of the glove box. On that door, in black script ink, was a signature. It was Henry Ford II's!

Josh asked, "Do you think that will make it worth more?"

Now who was surprised?

They had the complete car, although in pieces, and the skill, and from what I could see, the time and now resources to put it all back together.

This wasn't winning the lottery. But to them it was a miracle that just might put them, at least, back in the driver seat of their lives.

CHAPTER 6

Nasa Bound, But That Damn Thing Stays Here

*W*e set out from home this morning so we had a very nice homemade dinner and rest last night. As much as I love traveling, I still like sleeping in my own bed. Plus, we can just get up and go. We each have a "go" bag near the door so to be ready if we take either her car or my truck, in case we decide to stay out a few nights. We're prepared if we are onto something of a find, or if we just want to keep going in the same direction. No breakfast this morning, but Pat has her 55 gallon drum of coffee.

We are headed northwest today, driving along the Mississippi River and hoping to find some interesting stories around the Illinois Iowa border. We have found that getting back in the river bluffs and up on the hills allows us a better chance for some of these finds. The river up here runs out of her banks and quite often takes farms, homes and memories with it to be deposited somewhere else downriver only to become someone else's memories, most always devastating.

Today we headed for Keokuk Iowa. We would scour the eastern side of the river in Illinois. There is a lot of very nice scenery up here and we love to soak it all in. I have traveled almost all of my life and I just love seeing new things near and far from home. Some of my favorite trips involved flying into a country where I was not familiar with the language or culture. Luckily, I would always arrange for a friend who was local to the region to help me out, if one was near.

One particular time while visiting Dubai where I had a business partner, I was being chaperoned by his wife, their two young boys, his mother and two Philippine nannies. The wife was the only one that spoke English and that was a third or fourth language for her. They had a very large SUV so we loaded up everyone, baby supplies and two off-road strollers. They wanted to take me to the "bazaar" out in the desert. It took quite some time to get there so we left very early to arrive about 10 AM local time. When I saw this place, I could not believe it! There were huge tents. Huge buildings, the parking lots were acres and acres. I was told that close to 100,000 people a day show up here! No public transportation either, everyone drove their own Porsche, Masseratti, Bugatti, Ferrari and whatever other exotic car you could think of. The Mercedes Benz were usually left to the soccer moms' echelon. I actually saw a guy in a white kandora, the traditional white robe that men of the Middle East wear, walking his tiger! A FULL GROWN TIGER! I stayed away as that thing looked sleek, mean and hungry. It is always amazing what I see in the Middle East.

One other day when I attended a race at the Dubai AutoDrome at the invitation of Karim who was also on the racing board of Porsche. He owned quite a few and always did very well in the area rankings.

So much so, that his car was always shipped back to Munich after each race in its own shipping container of course, to be ready for the next race. One day I was wandering the pits, Karim, always the gracious host, was introducing me to all of his associates and friends. I remember one particularly HOT afternoon hanging on the fence watching some time trials of the motorcycles and Karim said, keep your eye on the green motorcycle, you remember Omar Mohammad, whom I introduced you to at the BMW pit. His full name is Omar Bin Osam Bin Mohammed bin Awed bin Laden. Yes, sometime in 2010 in Dubai the United Arab Emirates, among all of the other royalty that I was not aware of when I was meeting them, I had met one of the sons of the most infamous people of all time. Well back to our trek with the ladies. We got to the Bazaar, found a parking spot somewhere near Saudi Arabia and caught a shuttle to the main entrance. We drove past brand new barracks after barracks built for the Pakistani workers who were imported to do the menial everyday workman's tasks.

In this World Bazaar, every country in the Middle East was represented in their own compound. There were vendors of every nature and kind of things that you would expect to see. Not a tourist trap operation either, It was all first class. Fine leathers, silks, jewels, you name it they had it. There was a full-blown carnival in one small area. Hundreds of restaurants. There was a moat around the vendor village. Did I mention that there were a LOT of people? All wearing their native clothes. Luckily I have clothes that I had bought in Germany and had a European look rather than American, so I did not stick out like a sore thumb. On the drive over, I had mentioned that I would like to buy something for my wife to take home to her. As we all got out of the car and got the kids situated in the

SUV-SIZED STROLLERS, we were huddled up and I was told in no uncertain terms to never open my mouth and speak. Smile, nod yes or no, but never speak.

"Uh, what would happen if I were to come here alone?" I asked.
The reply was, "Oh, you'd just disappear." And dismissed with an upward wave of the hand while shaking her head no......
Ok, no talking, I got it.

We spent the day walking around the desert bazaar, even the tents were air conditioned. The smell from all the different ethnic cultures' cooking all blended together to make you constantly hungry, and we ate, and ate and walked it all off and started over. At this time, even though I had been with the family for a week, the two Philippine nannies had yet to speak to me. They were both small girls, maybe just in their early twenties. Lots of quick glances and giggles were their interaction with me, until we got to a very large bottleneck leading into some other area. The tents were situated to funnel everyone down to a single line passing through some kind of detector I would imagine. There were a LOT of people around us.

Now Grandma was in the lead with the wife giving instructions to her in German as to where we were going, the twin strollers were being pushed by the girls and I was in the rear. As crowds go, this one was very well behaved, however the children and I slowly became separated from our group. I was tall enough, by a head at least, to see every one of them ahead and Grandma and Mama anxiously looking over their shoulders as we began to stretch out behind them. I saw the worried look on their faces and decided to "help", a little. I managed to push my way up between the two strollers where I took the back of one and lifted it. Then I grabbed the front of the other, lifted it and just proceeded to plow my way through (the American way) with a lot of grunts and shouts of "Entschuldigung" (Excuse me in German). Well, the strollers, the boys, the girls and I made our way through the bottleneck with ease and we were all soon a reunited family once again. With their usual giggles and pointing the two nannies managed to squeak out a little English after they spoke to Mama. They said, "Herr Zimmer, it is so very good to have an American friend." A smile by me to them made another bond between cultures. That made me feel good.

Having been a member of Rotary International for over 20 year, I have come to understand the bonding of cultures. Rotary impresses on its' membership the foundation of reaching out and making friends with everyone that you can, through individual and group travel to exchange cultures and bring something home with you every time you travel. It became very apparent to me early in life that it would be very difficult to go to war with a nation if you were indeed friends with them on a business level as well as a personal level. Rotary sponsors youth exchange groups all throughout the year which entails a group of high school students from Illinois for example, exchange places with a group of students from Frankfort Germany for example. These groups leave for a year and stay with volunteer "homes" with parents and other children. You have to really want to do this and there are a few every year that find "homesickness" just too much to overcome. Rotary can take these children into account and either let them stay awhile to work it out, or go back home if the issue is just too much to overcome. My home has welcomed about 6 exchange students over the years and my son Nicholas went to Germany with one study group.

Much closer to home at the present, Pat and I had finished watching a barge exiting the lock at Keokuk and we headed east to see what we could find here in Illinois now. Since it was lunch time, we stopped at a farmers grill on the outskirts of a little town we were passing through. We both eyed the special of the day, chicken fried steak and mashed potatoes with gravy, but in the menu Sandwich section, it had BLT $6.75 and then right under that, it had BLT $7.75 which Pat caught with her eye for detail. Pat asked the waitress, "Now, I'm all for more is better, but why is the bottom one a dollar more?" The waitress said with a grin, "that was SUPPOSE to say BLT+Club for $7.75 but I had already printed them dang things twice and I wasn't about to do it again and just said the heck with it, I'll just explain it each time somebody asks. You are only about the one millionth who pointed that out!" She said with a wink. As usual, we had just had to query her about any interesting stories that might be hidden behind the cobwebs in some old barn. Without missing a beat she said "the Demont's have some weird stuff. Stop by and ask for Glenn, he runs the place now, but his second wife Barb has the stories." I paid the tab and since she wasn't sure I understood the directions she had just given me, she drew a map on the back of my bill. Go straight down Main, until it merges into the State Highway and take it seven miles and look for the driveway on the right side, right after the bridge.

Bingo, just as advertised, "Demont" written right on the mailbox. We turned in and parked right behind a huge pickup truck with duallies and large chrome stacks running up each side of the pickup cabin. I carry a supply of Gay Pride bumper stickers with me for just this type of meeting. Yep, I placed it about 4 inches down on the passenger side front bumper. He'll never see it for months. Now, getting back to our regularly scheduled program; It was about 2 PM now and I could see some activity out back. A group of people were hoisting a large well casing to be lowered down into a well. That would make sense since the big pickup said "Forney's Well Service". As I walked up, I waited around until there was a lull in the activity. "It looks like it's all under control now" I said to the guy who had the name "Digger" on his shirt. By that time, I guess Mr. Demont figured I was not with this crew and asked what I wanted. I followed him as he walked away trying to keep me from distracting an hourly crew. I thanked him and told him that I respected his time.

"I am a writer and I was sent this way via Betty down at the diner." He wiped his brow with a blue bandana he pulled from his back pocket. I introduced myself and the project. "You mean that damn....... THING?" He asked? I looked around and said, "well that's as good a start as any, yeah, that damn THING!" Thinking this would be a game where I could eventually figure out what the damn THING was and if it had any actual value to us.

Pat had joined us now and I introduced her. "Glenn Demont" tugging his hat.
"Would you have some time to tell us about... uh, the uh, you know…." and he interrupted with; "That damn thing!?"

Pat told him a little more detail about our project, in that we were looking for odd barn finds. Things that have no reason to be in a barn but were anyway, and that we wanted to write about them before they disappear.

Glenn seemed to think a little bit and decided that he could spare some time. Before he did, he yelled for Barbara, whom we were guessing was his wife.

"Barb knows more about this damn thing than I do, so we'll just get her to tell you about it." Barb was a match for Glenn. There were some introductions and small talk. She was no-nonsense and let us know that they were busy running a working farm. We acknowledged that and suggested that we could come back at a better time. She looked at us as she dried her hands off on her apron and announced, no, let's go on in there now and get to it.

We walked a ways past a few outbuildings, into the barn. She told us to wait there. I heard an engine start and here she came out on "Gator". This 4 wheel farm implement looked fairly new, but before we could say anything she saw the disappointment on our faces and said "This ain't it. We need to go down to the old barn." So with renewed curiosity we got on...and hung on! Boy, she knew how to drive this one! Down a path and through a pasture, up a hill and we were soon riding the ridge line with the warm fall wind in our faces, a trail of dust and leaves blowing behind.. We got a good view from up here and we could see a large plot of an unworked farm in the distance. We made a few turns and up and down a few more hills until we came to an old dilapidated shack and an old barn, almost falling down. We pulled up to it and got off. There was little sign that this place had seen any "farming" for quite some time. We followed her inside and could see the outside almost as much as if we weren't inside. There was a large piece of equipment covered in a few different old tarps.

"Well, here it is," she announced.

"What is it?" Pat asked.

"It's my daughter's. She wouldn't let us sell it. She won the damn thing and wanted it. No arguing with her. It was hers, she won it and we were keeping it. That's what it is."

She could see our confusion mixed with interest. "No one is interested in it. Now or then, but we kept it."

"It looks like a carnival ride," Pat said as we all started to pull the tarps off. Dust was flying everywhere, everyone was coughing and sneezing by now.

This looked like a rocket ship. Not a NASA rocket, but a full size cartoon-like rocket ship! It had Kraft Jet Puffed printed on the side of it in big red letters just like a Kraft marshmallow bag. The hull was white with highlights of blue. There were simulated exhaust port nozzles on the back side and the front came to a nice shiny point with an antenna, now quite bent. The damn thing was mounted on a semi truck trailer with all tires flat due to rot or some animal gnawing on them.

Well, I remembered as a kid that Kraft had a contest back in the late 1950's or 60's. To enter you had to write an essay about the future of the space age, and of course enclose some part of a bag of Kraft marshmallows. This was before I was in the essay writing business, but I did follow that contest. Recently I even looked it up on the inner-webs, and sure enough I found it, I placed a Facebook shot of it on my old high school's Facebook page. Back in the day, I think every kid in the country probably entered the contest.

Now Barb took over the narrative:

"My daughter Norma was still in elementary school and entered this contest in 1959. We were all surprised when we found out that she was in the top 10 entrants with her essay. I helped her a little, driving her back and forth to the library that year. She was always very interested in science. I remember she watched all the movies about space travel when she was a young girl and unlike others, really didn't have any need for dolls, no matter how I tried. She was bound and determined to be an astronaut." I interrupted and asked if she had followed through and become one. Barb said no, and before I could say "too bad", she told me that Norma had gone on to study meteorology and astronomy and did land a job at NASA where she had retired a couple of years ago.

Barb continued. "We were following the progress and were happy to see that the first prize was not just this monstrosity, but that the final winner would have a choice of this or $2500 cash money. We all assumed we would get the cash and that this damn thing would stay with Kraft for whatever reason. We were wrong. When she was announced the winner, they flew her and the family to New York for the big ceremony. Now up until this point, we were all thinking that the $2500 would go towards her college fund. When she got up on the stage, and they put the microphone in front of her, she let loose with this big story about bringing this damn thing back home and she would be the star of the show, giving lectures about space travel and then a tour of "space travel" on her very own rocket ship to whom ever would sign up for the ride."

"Well, there it was, for all the world to see. It was hers and it was coming back here. She had a lot of fun with it. I could hardly look at the neighbors knowing that we were, and were going to be the butt of their jokes for a VERY long time. I mean, just look at that thing! It has about as much business being up here on our farm as…." Barb was sputtering pretty well at this point, so we just looked at the ground, shook our heads in agreement all the while biting our tongues so as to not let the faintest bit of a snicker pass our lips.

Glenn had a pad laid for the damn thing and wired it up with a couple of the people from Kraft, all the while Norma supervising every bit of it. Why, she even slept in it most every night that first summer. And true to her word, she had the kids from 2-3 counties around here, all standing in line to take a turn sitting in it. It has 5 seats with seatbelts and helmets for each astronaut as she called them, an intercom with headsets so that they could all speak with each other, and an 8 millimeter projector that showed them blasting off into the wild blue. This was not a flight simulator like most people might think, but more of a glorified carnival ride. Pretty soon the novelty wore off.

Then high school started and, try as she might, Norma just could not get the school administration to see this as anything more than a carnival ride. Then she got a boyfriend and well, she just lost interest in the damn thing. She still had a very keen interest in science and space exploration, but after she was in her junior year, well she just wasn't interested in that darn thing anymore.

We had to put a fence around it because it had become quite a target for the kids around here sneaking in at night and painting it with different high school colors depending upon who was involved in the football championship that year.

We wanted to get rid of it and Glenn threatened to dig a hole, run over it a few times and push it in with his D9 one afternoon, but it was hers and her dream.

Sometime in the 70's after she had graduated from Northwestern, where she finished pre-med and was about to go to med school, she decided that she wanted to study meteorology and got a masters from the University of Wisconsin in Madison. She had a great imagination and finally got a job teaching and research at the Science Center in Huntsville Alabama.

After four years she got her doctorate in astrophysics back at Madison and went to work in Houston with great references from the RedStone Arsenal in Huntsville.

More than a couple of times Glenn threatened to put it on a trailer and take it down to NASA and leave it in their parking lot, but Barb was able to talk him out of it each and every time.

"So there Norma sat in all her glory at the Space Center in Houston and here we sit with this damn thing."

But, I have something left over here. You see, I spent some time in Madison Wisconsin and I didn't want to interrupt the flow back there but: I have spent some time at the University of Wisconsin at Madison. My father, as a Professor at the St. Louis College of Pharmacy had is opportunity to take his family to different colleges around the US during the summers. We spent one summer when I was probably 12 years old up there. They put the family up in a dorm room, then my father went off to attend conferences about teaching, pharmacy and education. There were things for the family to do and things for the women as well as the kids. Now this was where I found out that my parents style of parenting for me was the "feral version" and this was great for me. I would wind up with other kids separated form their homes and friends for the summers. It was soon easy enough to locate just the right kids and get them running with me. We would have fun running thought the crafts rooms they had set up for us. We especially liked the elevator races we had in the dorms.

Until we got caught.

It seems when all the elevators are commandeered by some wild little vandals from another town, there was a quick meeting and they rounded up the few ringleaders whom they could identify, and yes, I was one.

I don't think that they told my father that he would have to take his family home, but what ever they told him, I was promptly put under full house arrest.

For a 12 year old.
Not too bad.
They had a graduate Program that was doing some sort of study with feral children and we were more than welcome as an addition to their study (experimental) group. No real bad memories or scars, so I guess I came through without any trauma......

CHAPTER 7

The Bronze Rocket

It has been a while since we have been working on our project. This has been a wedding year for Pat and me, our daughter was married this July. We have not been following our plan at this point as many other issues took precedence.

I woke up this morning and suggested that we take a ride up into northern Illinois and get back into our routine. It was welcomed with open arms. I love traveling to someplace where I have no idea where the destination will be until I get there. So it happened in a small northern Illinois town this fall afternoon. The town square had the county courthouse right in the middle as you would expect, the buildings around the town square were all facing the courthouse and offered a beautiful little walk around it. A nice little coffee house was spied first by Pat, so we found a place to park and wandered in. It must be trial day because the place was full of people with lanyards around their neck which declared "Juror". Now in a friendly little town in the middle of Illinois, this presented a bit of a problem as EVERYONE is friendly and will wave and say hi to everyone. It's just a natural thing to do. We found a couple of little chairs outside, so we ordered our coffee and espresso along with a biscotti and sat down to do some major people watching. It must have been a pretty serious trial as there were a couple of deputies or sheriffs escorting this group of jurors around making sure nothing but a small wave or smile were exchanged. I waved, nodded and winked at many of them just to keep the local police on the ball. We were pretty far off the beaten path or interstates as they are now called. But thinking back on it, Highway 66 was always thought of as the Mother Road and we were a pretty far distance from there as well.

The barn we saw was rather ordinary and fitting of our goals for today; the first one we saw after hitting 240 miles. I turned into the driveway and we immediately saw that this was vacant and not receiving visitors as the "No Trespassing" sign informed. Not a stranger to having been chased off of a property in my younger days, encouraged by a shotgun of course, I thought it was time for an executive decision.......We left.

Since that approach yielded no real results we were back to the eyeball and binocular program. I looked at the near stuff with my eyeballs and Pat looked at the far stuff with the binoculars. This always seemed to get us results, even if one is a bad case of motion sickness for the one using the binoculars. It always amazes me at the number people who do NOT know how to use (focus) binoculars properly. So, I'll take a few lines her to describe the process. You can skip to the next paragraph at this point. Binoculars obviously have two separate optic system to allow each eye to to focus on a distant object. I first insist that you put the strap on over your head to keep from dropping them. You wouldn't believe how many people have dropped mine or knock them hard enough to cause them to need be sent back to the manufacturer for an alignment. Ok, hold them to your eyes. The first adjustment is to hold each side of the binocular with each hand and while you are looking though them, use your hands to push the two pieces together. There. You probably didn't know that they would move or why they should. You need to adjust them so that each eye is able to see directly through so that you really only see the field of view as one complete circle and not two separate circles. This is the first adjustment that EVERYONE forgets. If I see someone just pick up a set and start to look through them without setting this adjustment, I pretty much know that they have never seen anything through a set of these and are missing out on a lot. Now, after you get that part done, if you look around each eyepiece, you will see one with a set of numbers or dots that indicate the center and go from 0 to plus 3 and 0 to -3. You will now find that you can rotate these and there is also a reference dot right under these numbers. Go ahead and rotate this top ring so the the 0 is right above the single dot. If the left side has the ocular with the adjustable numbers, close your left eye and look through the rights side while you use the center focusing ring to bring a distant object into focus. If the right side has the ocular with the adjustable numbers, then close your right eye and look through the left side and use the center focusing ring on the binoculars to bring a distant object into focus. Now, leave the center focusing ring alone and open both eyes to view through the binoculars and twist which ever eyepiece has the adjustable ring on it to bring the distant object into focus. It may take a few times to find the focus point for you to comfortably view through the binoculars. Take a look at the number you have on the adjustable eyepiece as you can just dial this in like a pro the next time someone hands you a functioning pair of binoculars. By the way, if you are ever using a pair of binoculars, and you cannot get anything in focus this way and you feel like you are going cross eyed, put those down because they are seriously OUT of adjustment and need to be repaired. Happens more times than you would imagine. Well, I hope that this helps. Now, we will join our already continuing program.

Shortly, Pat spied a rather nice place through the hills and naked trees. We drove around the county for a while before we were able to get to the property's entrance. There were no signs of the anti-trespassing nature so we followed the driveway up to the house. It looked like a beehive of activity as we passed a couple of trucks coming down the drive as we were entering. When we got to the home, we could see that this must be moving day, or a moving week to be exact.

The first person to see us was a grey-haired gentleman that would fit the farmer identity. Tall, red and black flannel shirt, jeans and work boots. He was the owner, Levi Broadview. He looked cheerful enough considering nobody in their right mind should be happy on a moving day. We introduced ourselves and apologized for showing up unexpectedly on moving day. He explained that this was just downsizing as he is retiring from farming and that he and his wife were doing what they had always planned.

We explained our project and as Pat explained our interest in his barn or more importantly any hidden story, he chuckled and said, "Well, you caught up with me" as his outstretched hands signified he half expected us to be carrying handcuffs. He realized that his joke went over our heads and backed off that tack. He pointed over to his barn and started walking as he talked.

"Yeah, you might say that there's a hidden story in there alright. Goes all the way back to 1963. I was just a kid back then. Do you folks want to hear about it now or see it, or what? `` he asked "How does this work?"

I said this way sounded just fine as we continued walking. As soon as we got near the barn we could see a box van with ramps leading down to the ground from its deck. In the barn I could see a bronze-colored futuristic looking car. I stumbled as I was looking forth and back at the car and the truck and figured it was going with them. I mentioned that and Levi said,"No, it's going home." Before I asked another question, I decided to let him talk.

"I saw this car in town when I was still a kid, probably about 20-21 years old at the time. I was on leave from the Air Force and had traveled home to see my parents. I had just gotten off the bus and was crossing the street when this car flew by me. I ran after it for a few blocks, just catching up to it before it would spool up and pull off. I remember the cool sound it made when that turbine spooled up. I was hooked" he said.

By this time we were all standing in front of a 1963 Chrysler Turbine car. *The Bronze Rocket, The Root beer Jet, That Noisy Car, That Jet Car Thing.* It had all sorts of names, and it looked brand new!

It turns out that Chrysler and others had been developing a turbine powered automobile since the 1930's. Levi explained that the car was one of 55 produced by Chrysler, 5 prototypes that were all different versions and 50 production models in 1963 and 1964. All 50 of the production models were exactly the same. The same color scheme and the same options. They were given free to 203 different people to drive for a few weeks before turning it over to its next handler. These cars were driven in 133 different cities around the continental USA in that time to test their reliability and to see what kind of reception the general population would have upon seeing and driving one. The goal was to amass over one million miles on these cars and then analyze the data from each and decide whether or not to continue with the program.

Levi continued, "Who would have expected that an ordinary, middle class person in this small town would have the chance to drive a futuristic Turbine Car? This country is great! I never got to drive it or even sit in it as a passenger back then, but it stuck in my mind.

As an A&P (Airframe and Powerplant) mechanic at Chanute AFB, I had some free time and flight benefits. I found out about the turbine car and my CO at the base shared my enthusiasm and even encouraged me to find out about it. He was very interested in it as well, being a test pilot for years. He drove a very nice robin's egg blue Ford T-bird, a 1955 I think."

"With a few connections during and all through the Air Force, I was able to get a job in the Chrysler Turbine program as soon as I got my DD 214. They had an office waiting for me. My CO's letter of recommendation and my knowledge of turbines as taught by the Air Force, put me way ahead of *any* class of graduating mechanical engineers.

Unfortunately, I got into the program and found out later that same year that they had collected all the data and the cars were being brought back to the plant in Detroit to await further disposition."

Being in the military, Levi knew what that meant. He found that the data from the cars was being compiled and evaluated. Through a little more snooping, Levi figured out that if the data was good, the program would be upgraded, production cars would be refined and finally sold to the public. If the data was bad, and advance word was this was the case, then the program would be scrapped. In either case, however, these first 55 cars would be destroyed as per company policy! The only word that I can come up with to explain the look in Levi's eyes even now was just "INCREDULOUS"!

We were now sitting on a couple of hay bales that Levi had pulled up as he watched Pat and me take turns sitting in first the driver's seat and then the passenger seat before we would walk around looking at the lines, the chrome headlight bezels, the recessed rear tail lights, the chrome strips, the black vinyl top and the very distinctive stainless steel thrust port on the very center of the back of the vehicle.

He opened the hood and explained the development of the Chrysler A 831 Turbine Engine and then the development of the Body by Ghia of Italy and how they were handmade and shipped to Detroit for assembly into what you see here. Levi went on to explain that the rumor was that the car's body would have such a high import tariff that they had to be destroyed, but Levi assured us that just was not the case. It was just corporate policy and as silly as it sounded, it was to be followed.

Getting back to the data, it was not good. The faults found in this 2 year public test was that the 8 step starting sequence (remember that this is a real jet turbine) was just too complicated and wound up destroying the engine if not followed to the letter. "Did I mention that these cars cost Chrysler between $50,000 to $55,000 each to produce in 1963?" Levi added.

Other insurmountable problems were the very poor acceleration. Poor fuel economy was also listed, and this was a vehicle that could burn almost any fuel, tequila - no kidding the President of Mexico asked if one could burn tequila and after a short meeting, the engineers agreed and he did it. It could burn JP4 (jet fuel, of course) but not the most available fuel around at the time; regular leaded gasoline. It turns out that the lead would create particulate matter that would interfere with the precision tolerances in the engine. But the big fault was this: it was too noisy. Although the turbine was noted for its exceptionally smooth operation, passengers thought that the interior was too noisy. This was finally determined to be the tire noise, which could now be easily heard because there was no engine making mechanical noise and the turbine itself was so very quiet.

The plus side of the data proved that the engine had very high reliability, could use a variety of fuels, even perfume (although not cost effective) and had very low maintenance requirements.

Well, that was it. The entire lot of them were to be systematically destroyed. Levi had access to these cars in his position at Chrysler and would be seen driving his own brown Plymouth Valiant forth and back in his daily checks of the system.

Then one day he got an idea. He started changing and modifying his Valiant to look as much like the Bronze Rocket as he could. He even got a friend to paint it according to the exact paint code he got from the files. He was also seen taking one of the cars back through security every once in a while so his crew could do some final inspections.

As the destroy date got closer and closer, Levi and his crew found more and more information that needed to be checked on these cars, until, one day, Levi drove his car in and drove out in one of the turbine cars, right past the guard who waved him right on by.

He made it out that night, drove it to a secluded spot and drove it right up a ramp into a waiting red and white, U-haul box truck. He drove the truck back to his home and left it parked on the street. He began to drive his wife's identical Plymouth Valiant to work and back.

On the day that the cars were to be demolished, his check list showed that the 5 prototypes had already been shipped, 9 others were marked for private disposition or museum destinations. When it came time to get the somewhat similar, somewhat different Plymouth Valiant on the car trailer, even though there was notice by the hauler, Levi slipped him two 50 dollar bills with a wink. "One for you, one for the guy on the other end" said Levi with a wink. Must have worked. Go figure!

That weekend Levi drove the U-haul down to his parents house where he unloaded the car and parked it in the garage.

Time wore on, his family grew, the kids, one by one left the roost and married. Levi left Chrysler and found a small farm in northern Illinois for his family to be close to his parents. By the late 1990's nobody remembered anything about a Chrysler project car with a turbine engine and he would be seen driving it on certain occasions, but only rarely, and never anywhere that a crowd might form. Levi had his secret and even under the family's collective noses, no one suspected any grand theft auto or corporate espionage.

No, as Levi tells it now, pretty much everyone who was involved in that program is long gone or dead. He found a kindred spirit at a Chrysler reunion up in Ypsilanti Michigan a few years ago and they arranged for the car to be sent back to be displayed at an automotive museum with little to no questions asked.

You see, the statute of limitations expired decades ago. Levi's lawyer checked.

CHAPTER 8

The East
St. Louis Mob

*N*ormally we just stay inside during days of inclement weather, and this day you could certainly call inclement. I have never seen any "clement" weather anyway. It snowed yesterday and again last night. Now usually we would just adjust our plans accordingly, (pull the covers up over our heads) but like all good midwesterners, a little snow is all the more reason to get out in your vehicle. Most people are on the lookout for bread, milk and eggs. Why anyone would want to make french toast when it snows is beyond my logical skills. I won't lie, I am usually out on a liquor run. So we did have more than ample reason to be out driving about.

I had an idea that since there was an old race track in Granite City, we might scour some farm fields and barns in that area. Who knows, there might be a very interesting car or truck around the area.

Urban sprawl had pretty much taken over this area in Madison County, I hadn't factored that into the equation. Although Granite City Raceway had been there since I can remember, and Gateway International Raceway had built a new track and grandstand within the last 20 years, the few farms that were left had all been either consolidated or picked over. There was just nothing out there to get excited about. I stopped at what looked like an older gas station and started talking to one of the older looking patrons that was inside staying warm. After sharing the space heater, both warming our hands, I mentioned that, as I recalled when I was a kid, there were at least a few junkyards and stations that supported the old race track and had some interesting cars scattered around. He reminisced a while with me and then seemed to remember an old farm out of Fosterburg Road where I might be able to find some interesting things. It seems that there was a drag strip out there in the 1960's I had forgotten about. Big Daddy Don Garlits had raced there as well as many others. Well, this was all we needed and decided to call it a day. We did have a lead and it would be researched, in full, when the weather was less than inclement.

Life goes on.

I had not forgotten about the Fosterburg lead and that following spring, coming home from the racetrack one day (horse races) I was driving down Fosterburg Road and saw an old farmer standing by his mailbox sorting through his day's mail. I pulled into the driveway and introduced myself.

"John Hoffman" he said as he reached out his hand for mine. "What can I do ya for?' He asked. The introduction about my book is now pretty much implanted in my head, but I took caution and decided to play it by ear and just give him the facts as he needed them. I could tell that John appreciated that and that he wouldn't mind having someone to talk to for a bit. "Let's go on up to the house", he said, and then asked; "Where are you coming from?" I told him Tuesday was my day at the track. I couldn't tell if he would be offended as a protestant or offended as a Baptist. Not offended at all. He was horse people too as he accepted my ride back up to the house.

When we reached his house, I shoved it in park and looked around as he was still occupied with some piece of mail he received. We got out and I looked at his house. It had seen better days, and could at least use a coat of paint, but he seemed happy enough here.

"It's over there", he said, pointing to the barn. We walked into one of the most over-packed, stuffed-full-of-junk, barns that I have ever been in. There was nowhere to walk. We could just stand in the doorway and look at stuff. "It's over there in the back" he said while climbing over all manner of crap. Plows, tools, horse collars, an anvil laying on its side with a pile of horseshoes next to it. Piles of tractor parts, fenders, an engine laying dismantled from maybe the Vietnam War!?! I mean there was lots of "stuff" and as we got to a clearing, I could see the low silhouette of a sports car.

"What is it?" I asked. "It's a champion. A winner that's for sure, My son raced it around the SCCA circuit back in the 60's and 70's." Before I could ask for more details, he was pushing things and tossing others until we were standing next to it. It was a silver and black Porsche 914-6 according to its markings. Mid engine.

"My son Jack grew up on the farm and after he got back from the service, sort of tooled around here and there, you know, not much direction, didn't really know what he wanted to do. I sent him down to talk to a couple of my brothers in St. Louis. Paul was a pilot in

WWII and impressed Jack with a lot of stories about the glory days of flying. According to Paul, though, those days were fast coming to an end. Now my brother Art who went to pharmacy school in St. Louis told a different story and lit a fire under him. Art taught him something. He taught him how to study. Very simply he told him how to read what the teacher was teaching, and how to respond. It wasn't to just "parrot" the information back to him, but how to understand each teacher, what he or she felt was important and to use his brain to "think" like the professor and when asked a question, to search and remember what the teacher was saying and reading their emotions to find just that one correct answer that would satisfy the answer as related to the question. Seemed to do it. And well.

"Well, after that trip he came back with a different head on his shoulders. Turns out Art had the magic for academia and planted that seed in Jack's head. You know, Jack went to college and then borrowed money from me to go to dental school and became a dental surgeon. He started his own practice and within the year he came over to pay it back. He wrote me a check for the whole thing! I said, let's spread it out so you don't have to pay it all back at once. He looked at me and winked, 'It's no problem dad.'"

"Well he got to racing cars and he opened up one of the first Porsche-Audi dealerships in the Midwest. He practiced orthodontics and surgery, raced cars, had a car dealership and later, flew his own float plane up into Canada where he and his family built a little fishing resort.

"At any rate, that's all that's left of his racing days around here. He asked me to keep it down here. I think he wanted to keep it away so neither he nor his son could drive it any more." Then he looked around before he said to me. "Don't tell anyone," as he winked, "but I used to drive it years ago."

Now as you can see, this just wasn't much of a story at all. Certainly didn't really fit in with any of these others that I have collected so far. But Wait! There's more!

I looked around for more fodder. Like I said, there were lots of things in this barn. At times it looked like it was more of a very sloppy storage unit than a barn. It seemed that John just couldn't part with anything.

I had about given up when I saw a tarp covering some furniture in another area of the barn. As we made our way over there, John was explaining to me the fine points of a Ford 5000 tractor over a John Deere 2520 tractor. The differences now elude me. That's good for you. I guess I got finished listening before he got finished talking.

Now we were standing in front of a very dusty pile of furniture. It looked like something from the 1940's. High wingback chairs, dark mahogany woodwork. Fine embroidery and piping along the edges. Most of the chairs looked nice enough, however, a couple of them and a couch or loveseat had the stuffing torn out of them and looked like a bobcat had eviscerated them.

I mentioned that this could be a place to store some more "stuff" if he had a bonfire tonight. John turned and looked at me like I had committed the very first blasphemy in his brand new cathedral! And the lecture I got to go along with it would be enough to make a Catholic School boy enroll in a monastery.

Good thing I stuck around, this was one heck of a back story.

It seems that back when John and his wife had first bought this farm and had worked it for a few years, a neighbor had moved into the vacant house across the road. Being neighborly folks, John and his wife took a pie over to the new people on a Sunday morning after services. They seemed nice enough, but a bit standoffish, as you would expect a transplanted city couple to be out in a rural area. There was a faint idea in the back of John's head that he had seen this man before, although he wasn't certain where it might have been.

It wasn't too long before John remembered. His pictures had been in the papers many times. This new neighbor was the gangster Dinty Colbeck who ran a gang called Egan's Rats. As John told the story, back when he was growing up in Baden, in the northern reaches of turn of the century St. Louis, he had witnessed the robbery of the Baden Bank on Broadway in broad daylight! As a kid he wasn't pressed into serving as a witness, but he swears, and many others corroborated, that this was a job pulled by The Rats. John can't say for certain now that he saw or even remembers any details of that day, but he is still certain that it was Dinty running out of the bank with a sack of loot and a 32 revolver.

When John told me that story, I asked him if he told this to "Dinty" at any time during his residency there. John just gave me one of those knowing looks of *WHAT ARE YA, NUTZ?*

John continued with a story that begins on a snowy day when the country had recently entered into World War II. John had been given some information that the Goodyear tire store in town had received a limited lot of brand new rubber galoshes. During this time of rationing of gasoline and rubber, it seemed like an opportune time to get some new boots. Having lived through rationing with electricity and gasoline, I have at least a passing knowledge of how this can *alter* your character a bit

So here was John getting his mail, wearing his shiny, brand new boots, when Dinty comes out to collect his mail as well. At the time, John said it was a Saturday morning and some of Dinty's gang were with him. When Dinty saw his boots and asked about them, John told him and said that they had quite a few pairs if he wanted to go and get some. Dinty and his friends (Egan's Rats) thought this was a great idea and it was decided then and there that they would ALL go into town and get some boots. John was swept up in this and was included as a passenger to direct them to the proper merchant. I had a very hard time imagining John getting into a car full of St. Louis gangsters, any one of them could have committed at least a murder or two.

Every last one of them got their boots. John said that he saw at least one 38 caliber snub nose checked for fit down into and retrieval from these new boots along with a few knives, blackjacks and brass knuckles. On the ride back a bottle or two was being passed around the car and he felt that he should take a snort or two, you know, being neighborly. When the pulled up in the front of the house, they all sort of rolled out of the car and then one grabbed a hand full of snow and threw it. Well that's all it took. Here he stood in the middle of a bunch of notorious thieves, gangsters and murderers, John was in the middle of a snowball fight right in the middle of the road, including Dinty! John said he made sure his aim wasn't so good. One by one they made it back into the house where they had a full bar set up in the basement. Just like you would imagine an old time Chicago Speakeasy.

Fast forward to 1943 and Dinty was machine gunned down in his car crossing the Merchants Bridge in north St. Louis. There were territory wars going on all throughout Illinois. The Shelton gang at this time was out collecting new territories and a small act of just "crossing" a county line, much less a State line boundary as the Mississippi River could trigger a large war for this minor indiscretion. So, as was the custom in those days, the deceased was laid out in the living room of their home. John and his wife went to pay their respects. At some point Dinty's widow approached John and his wife and told them she was leaving the area and they could have their pick of anything in the house as she felt a special friendship with the couple. Now that is how all of this furniture wound up in John's barn.

But the story doesn't end there. Not with the German background of John Hoffmann and his Irish brother in law, Bob Courtney. It seems that the furniture was very nice and one particular chair found its way into the main house. As you would expect there would be a little drinking when the family got together…..and stories were told…... and embellished…….until one particular evening of "relaxation" John and Bob came up with the idea that since most of the money from the bank robberies, mail truck heists and especially the Staunton Post office heist which was hit for $55,000, was never found, it *MUST* be hidden in some of the furniture.

John said that he and his brother-in-law didn't do it right away, but thought about it over the years until one particular New Years Eve

Party, when the women were all in another part of the house, John and Bob got a carving knife from the kitchen and proceeded to "gut" that chair like two crazed outlaws who finally stumbled upon the "loot".

Only it wasn't there. By the time the wives found out what had happened, the two were on their way out to the barn intent on cutting open each piece of upholstered furniture and smashing each wooden piece until they found their treasure. Luckily, the wives ran after them hysterically screaming at them and intervened so that the rest of the furniture was spared. Again, not the end of the story.

It seems that each subsequent New Years Eve party would occur at the farm and one by one, every year, another piece of historic furniture was sacrificed. Women being the smarter of the two species, John's wife had the presence of mind to add this one bit of contractual discourse as a precursor to each party; no matter which piece of furniture you choose to "explore', you will agree to its complete reupholstery and rebuilding when you are finished.

And so, that is how John and his brother-in-law managed to destroy 6 pieces of fine and maybe historic furniture and have it replaced to its pre-War regalia.

As I was driving back home and especially searching through any new barn that may hide a special story, I wondered if I might have missed something by not asking that one more little question or if I was *nosey* enough.......I certainly do not want to leave anything behind.

CHAPTER 9

MGA and The Con

*W*e were driving down the road one day.........

Nope, not today. We tried an experiment last week. I went on Craigslist from southern Illinois and placed the following ad: *Do you have an interesting story involving something in your barn?*

WOW! You would not believe the responses that that ad brought out. It was a good thing that it was a blind ad.…It certainly saved me days of replying to them. We closed it down after a month because the amount of time it took to read through each would be more than just driving around and randomly knocking on doors like we had been doing.

However, one reply was worthwhile. We set up an appointment to meet Susan Meyers.

Susan lived on her family's farm in the Little Egypt area of southern Illinois and specifically in the Shawnee Nation Forest. We were able to plan a nice trip directly from our home to hers, something we have not had the pleasure to do since we started this odyssey.

It took us about two and a half hours to get to the farm. There was much beautiful scenery to take in on this early morning summer drive. We took a couple of interstates on this trip only to stay focused and not be distracted following a random lead. No, we had an appointment with an already pre-qualified lead.

Susan had told us first by email and then by a phone call about the car. It was a 1960 MGA Convertible. Brilliant Orient Red with a black top and white interior. It was the 1600 deluxe Roadster Mark II she said, sounding like she was reading it out of a brochure. I automatically asked if she was selling the vehicle, thinking this just might be a ruse to get me in front of her to try and sell it. She replied with a soft, "no, I….I could never sell it." That clinched it for me. Off we went.

As with many roads through southern Illinois, a lot of the farm houses seemed uncommonly close to the road. Almost as if the road was running through their front yard. You see, many years ago these farms were at a fairly large set-back from the main road with a nice long driveway back to the home and other buildings, but IDOT, (Illinois Department of Transportation) in their continuing improvement to move people from point A to point B and not paying attention to anyone or anything in between points "A and B" had widened these roads, increased them from two, to four and sometimes even 6 lanes with a large median and wide shoulders. The traffic that was once sparse and maybe half a mile away soon was running right past the front porch. It was a gradual creep, it didn't happen all at once. Most people hardly noticed it, except for the owners. You can imagine that there were many meetings, town halls and notices before any of these changes could and eventually would take place.

Once we had left the interstate highway system we were on our favorite way of traveling. The state highway system of each state should be identical, but they aren't. The chief engineer of each state has a way of putting their own touch to the roads. I don't profess to understand how to build a road, but it certainly appears to me that the majority of the budget allotted for the Illinois Highway Department get proportionately small the further you get from Chicago. The longer we drove south in this area, the more it seems that the roads are neglected. Driving 50 or 100 miles from an interstate highway, you will find yourself WAY out in the country and your eye better be on the look out for roadkill, deer, alive or dead, turtles and the occasional coyote.

We pulled up in front of the house and Susan was sitting on the front porch swing. She was older than I expected. Tall and thin when she stood, she was a very attractive woman. She wore a flowered blouse tucked into her khaki pants. Her long grey hair pulled up into a bun showing a few lines where either joy or sorrow had left them over the years. She wore no makeup except for maybe some natural lip gloss.

She walked down the three wooden steps to the yard, turned and walked towards the car, never letting her gaze stray from us.

She walked to the passenger side and greeted Pat first and then waited for me to come over and join them. We introduced ourselves in person now and shook hands as she offered hers first. We were invited back up to the porch to sit and talk. Susan and Pat sat. I stood on the second step with my hand holding the banister. She seemed very keen on knowing more about our book.

"Like I said on the phone, I am a private person. I don't know why I reached out to your ad on Craigslist. One of the ladies in my bridge club told me about it and thought that I should contact you. Mind you I have better things to do than to surf the 'net" she said. "Delores, one of the last of my dear friends, knows me so well. She knows the story and after a few conversations about it, convinced me that I should be able to tell the story and let others hear it."

"I don't know," Susan started, " I thought maybe they could learn something. Delores said, maybe they could be entertained…. She always was a smart…..", but she stopped before saying it and glared at me as if I had made some major faux pas, which I didn't understand at all. I looked around to see if there was anything I might deflect it off to, but no. I was holding it.

"It sounded like a very interesting vehicle from your description on the phone," I said, trying to change the subject or at least to help her remember that I was the one who made the initial contact with her. I mean, I ought to at least get some credit for that. No, she seemed much more at ease speaking with Pat and would only tolerate me as long as I was there.

"Come on." she said to Pat and walked towards the old barn. It was expected that I would dutifully follow…..maybe even keep my mouth shut.

She took Pat's arm in hers and walked toward the barn with me following. As they walked Susan was speaking about not having many visitors anymore, even though the new state road now runs right up her.……, and she didn't complete that thought out loud either, but Pat looked back at me and grinned.

When we all were finally inside the barn, the car was not in the back. Not under a pile of crap. Not even under a tarp. It was sitting in the middle of the barn as if it was a show piece. There was not a speck of dust on it. I remarked that she did not have to go out of her way to clean it up and display it for us. Again, a quick glare. Arrows could have shot out of her eyes at me, for all I know, they did. I wouldn't know, because I quickly sidestepped that glare and got to the other side of the car.

"This car always sits here! I dust it every morning and check all the wires, hoses and other rubber parts to see that the mice aren't getting to it." At that time I did notice an abundance of mouse traps all around the car; all with fresh dabs of peanut butter on the triggers. "Seems to me you need a cat or two," I said.

Oops, another mis-step. "There are plenty of cats in here" as she pointed to one of the worthless creatures sunning himself to sleep. "You know," Pat said, "why don't you go back into town and pick up that part you wanted and I can call you to come pick me up when Susan and I are finished." Susan Meyers seemed to like that idea. As I started to ask if they would like me to bring back lunch, Ms. Meyers admonished me that she was quite capable in preparing a meal or two. I assumed I would be eating alone in town.

"Great idea" I exclaimed. "Check your cell phone and see if you have ser….."
"Of course we have service out here." said Ms. Meyers, " What century did you drive in from anyway?"

"Later" as I quickly backed out and headed for the state road.......

I drove back to the closest town that I thought might keep me occupied for a couple of hours. There was no Walmart, but then, there is always a Walmart. No, I was looking for the main street running into town and was pleased to see that this one announced that it was an "Illinois MainStreet Town". This meant that it had passed a few qualifications to get it listed as such and thus was part of a group that was supported by the Illinois government for historical and economic development. In short, this means that the majority of the citizens of this community not only think that it is worthy of keeping, but are actively involved in making that happen. Volunteers run the program in each town, so I set off to find the office. However, lunch first.

I found the MainStreet office across the street from a nice little restaurant that was famous for its desserts. By-Right Desserts was run by a nice woman named Ann, who could not say anything bad about her town. I told her that I was familiar with the MainStreet community; I was a board member as well as President for the Alton Illinois program for years. Ann opened the door and whistled like a carny worker right before she yelled "HEY RUBE!" but instead she yelled "HEY CHARLENE!" Pretty soon a big hair, redheaded woman opened the door to the restaurant and looked around. Ann motioned her over to my table.

Well, she and Charlene were happy enough to meet me and made me feel like a VIP, (which I am not). I asked if they would join me for lunch and they agreed. We spoke about their town and my town. We all learned something about each other. After lunch I was invited back to the MainStreet office to be shown their local programs and projects, which were all very impressive. I was quizzed about our programs, which were quite a few years before theirs, as I was on the Alton Board in the mid 1990's when the group was just getting off the ground. After a tour of the town we retreated to the local watering hole, "Rapid Edwards", where I then asked them about Susan Meyers and her MGA. I got quite an earful and by the time Pat called me at 5:30, I felt that I had enough information to write my story. Bidding both Ann and Charlene goodbye, I found that the tab had been paid by Charlene. Nice group.

I rolled into the driveway about 6 pm thinking I probably should have gotten a room. No need. When I got to the Meyers farm, Pat was just saying goodbye and walked down to the car. Pat waved to Susan and Susan waved back. I waved and Susan yelled "Goodbye Pat". So much for my likable personality.

I told Pat that I had gathered a lot of information about Ms. Meyers and her car. So had Pat. We decided to drive back home and compare notes as we drove, all the while Pat writing her notes down and inserting anything relevant from mine. By the time we got home we were both confused as my story and hers were not at all parallel as they should have been, and intersected at only very basic points. We were ready for bed. Maybe a good night's sleep would make this clear in the morning.

We both went over our notes as the other listened to the story. I read through Pat's notes and she read through mine with no revelation. After much discussion, telling and re-telling the story as reconstructed from our notes, we came to the obvious conclusion that we each had bits of the real story and we might be able to sort through and get to the real story.

After quite a few rewrites and a couple of calls by Pat to Susan to clarify and verify the facts, we have reached the conclusion that follows. The only loose end we had was that Pat said that as she was looking at the car, and opened the glove box, she saw an old jar with a rusted top. Sort of like the little glass jars that those little Vienna Sausages came in. Except that this one had what looked to be some broken, yellowed teeth in it. Through the rust on the top of the jar Pat said that she could just make out the words "Sausage King". When Pat asked what it was, Susan said that she found it rolling around in the trunk one day and figured that they must have belonged to Christopher. Pat got the feeling she didn't want to talk about it, so she dropped it. See, some stories just have dead ends.

Susan Meyers was the daughter of Mickey and Claire Meyers who were married in Cuyahoga Heights Ohio in 1942. They were traveling musicians with some of the big bands around during the late 30's and 40's, but the war brought an end to that and since Mickey was too old to be drafted, the family subsisted on odd jobs around Cleveland. Susan was born in 1943. Try as they might, the Meyers could never get ahead of the bills. Sometime in the early 1950's Claire took off on her own leaving Mickey with a 10 year old girl to raise. With his skills honed by years of playing cards with the other musicians of the troupe, he found that he could bring home enough money playing cards after hours in the clubs around town. Susan learned to raise herself with a little help from Mickey when he was sober or awake which rarely coincided.

Some time when she was 13, Mickey got a line on a farm that could be had cheaply in southern Illinois, so they set off in their old Packard with their belongings to the land of Egypt. (Little Egypt Illinois is the land around the tip of Illinois terminating at Cairo, hence the relationship.)

Mickey had enough to purchase the land on a contract for deed. As long as he made the payments, he would eventually own the property, which was always his promise to Susan. He worked the farm and also hustled a few poker games as his old friends would drop by. Now he never hustled cards in Little Egypt, but would take his crew across the river to either Kentucky, Tennessee, or Indiana so as not to cause a problem at home. He was smart and stayed clear of the law although they were in some tight spots every once in a while.

The farm pretty much broke even until a geologist for an oil company knocked at the door. It seems that there was evidence of an oil deposit under their farm. Mickey agreed to let them explore and when they found enough evidence, they sunk five or six wells on the property. Each one paid off just enough to keep the contract for deed alive every year until the property was finally listed in Mickey and Susan's names.

With this new income, Mickey had more time to work the card hustle with his buddies. Mickey also learned about leases and found that he could lease out the ground to be worked by other farmers in the area and he would get paid for doing nothing on it! What a great deal! They were earning money off the crops that the other farmers tended and also getting income from the oil under the land! Susan had kept at her studies in school and graduated high school with honors.

Sometime in 1960, Mickey turned ill and was spending more time in the hospital than he was on the farm or on the road. Susan was taking over most of the business end of the property and learned to manage it pretty well with her father's tutoring. Mickey succumbed to throat cancer in 1964.

There was a very nice funeral, as he helped plan it, even had a fried chicken dinner at the Farmers Hall in town. While the community didn't know much about this family, they all rallied around Susan, now 22 and sole owner of this property. A few local men tried to date Susan, but she was never really interested in any of them. She ran the farm and even started hiring hands to run her own crops instead of leasing it out as Mickey had advised her to continue doing.

In 1965 a man pulled up the long driveway in a flashy European sports car. The driver of the red convertible flew up from the state road, got out, and dusted off his clothes before Susan had stepped into the yard to ask what his business was on her property.

Christopher Scott introduced himself as a business man who had a new project lined up from MIT that involved farm lands around the midwestern communities that were plagued with the problem of mine subsidence.

Now southern Illinois had long been mined for coal through strip-mining and anyone could see the obvious damage as small mountains of "tailings" followed any of these huge excavators as they scraped the top soil from the land to get to the coal located fairly close to the surface. From these piles, rain water would weep through and leach out all sorts of minerals and chemicals best left underground. Next to any of these hills, were pools of water that had run off the tailings and collected at their base. This water always had some strange color or characteristic; neon green, rainbow sheens, cloudy, murky, all the words that you would NOT want associated with your water supply.

As an alternative, a lot of Illinois communities had agreed to long wall mining under their property for a small mineral rights agreement. Long wall mining moved the actual operation of the strip mine back underground where the rape of the land could not be seen. No destroyed fields. No mountains of tailings. No green pools of odorous and questionable water. Everyone should be happy....... But they weren't.

Dr. Scott, yes, MD and PhD in physics from MIT, explained to Susan that he and his colleagues had been working on ways to keep these long wall mines from collapsing and rendering the lands not only useless, but very dangerous and costly. Susan became instantly interested. Although she still had a few pockets of oil remaining, she had been approached by more than a couple of mining companies wanting to explore for coal. She had held off the strip mining groups as it was very obvious that she didn't want to destroy her farm. But the long wall groups, well, they had made a pretty nice presentation each time, and the price seemed to keep going up with each. Now at some point, she must have realized that she might need to do something different and this sounded at least safe.

She invited Dr. Scott in to talk a little more. He did everything right, he had a business card, pamphlets and too many published white papers on the subject for her to read through and understand in her lifetime. Not that she couldn't, but they sure looked dry and boring.

Better to have an expert tell her what was in them than to investigate it herself. She said that she was interested in hearing more.

Dr. Scott said that although he was just passing through the area before going on to Vanderbilt University to give a lecture, he could stay in town tonight at the local hotel and have dinner with her if she wouldn't mind. She didn't.

Dr. Scott was not only educated, but stood well over 6 feet with broad shoulders, brown hair and a smile that made Susan's heart melt. Plus that car was nice. She offered to meet him at the hotel later in the evening, but she was really hoping that he would say that he would be happy to pick her up in his car.

Dr. Scott was on time and off they went, this time with the top up so as not to mess her hair. He knew these things.

At dinner they spoke about the project of long wall mines and how the land was left supported only by a few columns of coal. Imagine if you will, acres of empty caverns just under the farmed fields above, with just enough columns to barely hold up the leftover land. Earthquakes, which this area is prone to, could shake everything and drop the grounds 12-20 feet at a time. The land couldn't be farmed any longer and would probably just collect stagnant water for time immortal. That couldn't happen!

Dr. Scott and his team had developed a process that, unknown to anyone at the time, could reclaim this land by just filling the caverns to the top with regular water and their special concoction of gasses, the base being CO_2!! They had perfected a way with ultrasonic waves to treat the CO_2 that would allow it to actually vibrate each molecule in between the hydrogen and oxygen atoms and change the structure with an exactly placed electrical discharge of many thousands of coulombs that would instantly turn the concoction solid but permeable so it would act just as the ground and minerals it was replacing.

Now that they got that out of the way, they finished their dinner along with two bottles of Beaujolais that Dr. Scott had brought with him. The waitress hesitated at first, but decanted it after she spoke to her manager, who agreed that this was a much better wine than they had ever seen………in this town….EVER.

On the ride back, Susan convinced him to drop the top of the car for a nice summer night ride to her farm. She even convinced him to take the long way home, so that she might enjoy her wonderful night just a bit more.

When they finally got home it was well past 11 and he walked her to the door. She turned, and as she told him what a wonderful night she had, she placed her right hand above his heart and leaned in to kiss him on the cheek. Sensing this, he waited until her lips were almost on his cheek. He turned quickly and their lips touched. Surprised, but pleased, Susan closed her eyes and ran her hand to the back of his neck. After a few seconds, she pulled away and again thanked him for the evening and went inside, not ever looking back.

Dr. Scott stood there for a couple of minutes wondering what to do. Susan, equally wondering, stood silent behind the door, listening to what would happen next. Then she heard his footsteps going down the steps, his car door open and close and finally the car starting and driving off.

Susan was pleased with the evening

Dr. Scott was much more than pleased.

Over the next few months Susan and Dr. Scott saw much more of one another, There were phone calls and dinners, lunches and yes, overnights. Things had turned romantic over the summer as both of them had planned. Many evening drives which always ended up with each of them finding some way to entice the other into a rather passionate kiss which led to, well, you can imagine. Susan and Dr. Scott were an "item" soon seen all over town and throughout the community. She was with him as he pitched his process to the other farmers in the area. When asked if he ever travelled to other states, his answer was sufficient that Illinois was well stocked with long wall mines throughout the state. Southern Illinois just seemed to have a larger percentage of them. Talk turned to investors for this project and Dr. Scott seemed to be getting more concerned. Lack of worry or interest would equate to fewer people investing. Why, if the people that are suffering the most from this dangerous situation didn't think much about investing in it, then how serious might they be about even saving their farms?

One night the following spring, Dr. Scott appeared at Susan's door with a distraught look on his face. After much persuading, he grimly explained to Susan that the "One" farm that had the absolute worst case of mine subsidence had backed out of funding and being the showpiece of his project. Susan tried everything, (and she was clear about this, EVERYTHING) to ease his obvious distress, but nothing was helping until she asked if her farm might work as a showpiece. She also volunteered that she might be able to invest up to a hundred thousand dollars in the project. Dr. Scott was very reluctant to this idea at first. He told her how much he cared for her, and that he just couldn't bring himself to enter into a business relationship with her. Susan persisted, explaining to her "Darling Christopher" that theirs was a lasting love, and nothing would make her happier than seeing his project come to fruition. She was confident it would eventually provide a great return on her investment. Dr. Scott succumbed to her logic and charms, and spent the night happily in her arms.

The next day they took a long ride in the convertible, talking of their future, their future together. She loved their rides and he had even taken the liberty of leaving his convertible with her and would always return with a different car. She got accustomed to driving it around by herself after he had taught her how to use the manual transmission. She waved to everyone as she drove. The town was used to seeing her in the fire red convertible with her hair flying behind her as she sped down the local roads.

This morning Susan had a skip in her walk as she ran up the steps and opened her front door. She placed the daily mail on the back of a couch and turned as she heard his car come up the driveway and stop. Yes, she would invest $210,000 into the project, become a named investor for a 20% interest in the operation. Christopher said that he would have the papers drawn up tonight by his lawyer who was somewhere local in the area and be back in the morning to execute the transaction.

She hesitantly asked if she should write the check now, but felt very reassured when he laughed it off and said, "No, silly, I'll come by in the morning and pick it up." He would occasionally still take a hotel room in town when he had meetings to deal with, not wanting to burden his associates with the added drive out to her farm.

She was up bright and early the next morning and had breakfast all ready when Dr. Scott showed up. She met him at the door wearing a red and white checker pattern apron that, when she turned around, revealed she was not wearing anything else. Christopher scooped her up in his arms and kissed her passionately as he took her into the parlor.

Breakfast was cold but they ate it with a renewed energy, with at least one more interruption caused by their all engulfing passion. And a nap, which was ended by his latest growing passion…....

Dressed and fresh after a paired shower, they began talking about their future including the first hint of her much needed check. He wanted to make sure that she was indeed sure about this as she tore off the signed check. He was standing over her shoulder with a folder of documents that she needed to sign. She took them and said that she would have them looked over by her attorney before her signature, but before he could register his need to quickly proceed, she handed him her check. Once again smiling, he tucked the check in his wallet which he then put in the right inside pocket of his corduroy jacket. He stood there pensively for a moment, and then turned and waved as he walked out the door with a blown kiss and the promise to see her when he returned later that day.

When she returned from her meeting with her attorney she was not happy. The documents had more than a few glaring errors that had been pointed out. She had instructions of what to change and what were just elementary mistakes that any lawyer would flag, but nothing of any big worry, for she had assured the lawyer that this was indeed a valid business transaction and their relationship was its iron clad guarantee.

According to my sources in town, that was the last time that she ever saw Dr. Scott.

And the last time she ever drove the 1960 MGA Deluxe Mark II Roadster.

CHAPTER 10

Does a Server Farm have a Barn?

*T*his one started out as normal. I was driving and Pat was navigating. I noticed a large bunch of wires on one of the telephone poles on the road leading up to the farm house. We drove up to the house and politely knocked. A young woman holding a baby answered the door and we began to present our abbreviated pitch since she looked busy and harried as many young mothers look when someone invades their day.

Carrie Ruette was her name. Her husband was Oscar. She chuckled at the thought that she may have something of interest in her barn. Lets go talk to my husband she said, and off we went to the barn. Opening the side door, we were really surprised to find ourselves on the main floor of a modern day server farm. This was a full fledged, professional looking operation. There were rows and rows of computers in rack mounts with all the blinking lights, bundled wires, to go along with it. This was an environmentally controlled atmosphere with a very professional and secure main control room overlooking the entire operation from a slightly elevated vantage point with windows allowing visibility for 360 degrees from the center of the barn. The Mission Impossible set could have copied this place! Everything to be monitored of importance was with strategically big screen monitors readable from any spot in here. As a former techie myself, the very first thing that came to my mind was this was trying to be a one person operation if it wasn't already. Ok, all of my speculation was over;

What looked to be at least 100 servers all rack-mounted in this climate controlled, sterile environment. Cool, dry air circulated and the subdued lighting all added to the cool factor.

All of this seemed to be kept running by this one guy named Oscar.

Ok, it was a small operation, but even so, one tech and a new mother?

What is this?

Our suspicions that clued us were the amount of cables and fibers that seemed to be leading to this one small farm in the middle of nowhere. Certainly this was **not** the next silicon valley.

Now for the back story:

Oscar and Carrie Ruette were two, nice, millennials who had found a way on their own. They had met after college at a regional finance company in Chicago where they were both trudging through their day, just trying to make ends meet, Oscar as a techie and Carrie as a bookkeeper. Neither one particularly liked the job, but it did pay the rent. They had gotten married after a couple of years working there. They made a nice couple. They had a nice living and soon had a baby girl that they named Aurelia for some reason unknown to me. Keeping the books, Carrie was keen to notice the amount of money that the company was spending on rent. Not just physical buildings and storage space, but renting space to keep digital files. It seems that the finance industry takes up a lot of space for files which are farmed out to companies that just have an abundance of file space, bandwidth and speed. Carrie highlighted this each month as she made copies of the invoices and took them home to Oscar. With a few years worth of documentation of these 'rents', in front of them, spread out on the dining room table in their small, first floor, two bedroom apartment in Wrigleyville, they were overtaken with the absurdity of paying for space to keep invisible "bits". This was a point that they focused on with laser accuracy. A plan began to form, or "farm", to be exact.

They were very methodical, and had been planning on a home in the far west suburbs. But now, they were looking for a small farm, with some storage buildings. The plan was to start a server farm and rent out space to local companies around the area. This was a perfect plan, Oscar knew tech, Carrie knew the business. All it would take is a little capital to purchase the servers and digital storage, get a few customers and off they go, raising their kids at home, never having to get up and go into work and best of all, never having to answer to another boss again for the rest of their lives.

Finding the farm was difficult and at first looked like it would not happen. Every place they looked at was always first, too expensive and second, too big. Just as they were about to give up, a broker called with a little hobby farm with about 20 acres, a house, a newer barn and some out buildings. The only problem was that this was a couple hundred miles from Chicago and family. About the same time, Carrie saw an opportunity to snatch the server rental from the company that was now blatantly overcharging the finance company.

The costs of server "rent" had increased almost ten times since the finance company had started. At first the increases were small and since the company was small, hardly noticeable, however as the years went on and the company grew, their need for digital "space" also grew. Uncontrolled costs will surely sink any new company and the "suits" from within were more than pleased with themselves when Carrie and Oscar presented a plan to not only drop their server rental costs, but to rein them in and allow complete control with a local company.

Within a few months, Oscar and Carrie had finalized the sale on the farm, moved in and also closed the deal to host the rental of the finance company's files for a year with an option to extend it to five years after the first six months.

When the six months had timed out, the finance company executives decided that it was no longer interested in paying rent for its digital files and invested in its own small farm and placed it in the basement of a building the company owned on North Halstead Street in Chicago. They would "give' Oscar and Carrie the last 6 months of their contract as severance from the deal.

Now you would think that this would have been a financial disaster for Oscar and Carrie, had it not been for the fact that the finance company's original storage provider had pulled some shenanigans in its contract and legal documents. It seems that it had a rider in there that provided that, if the finance company sold or leased out the contents of this lot of storage, it was required to take a certain grandfathered lease with it. No one paid any attention to it over the years and as it turns out, that lease was making a nice bit of income for whoever was hosting it.

Trouble was, no one knew anything about this lease. Any documentation and information had been shuffled about many years ago in various mergers and acquisitions. The finance company was trying to do more IT work than it realized it could handle. Something had to give. As with all opportunities, one company's problems became another one's solution. After years of trying to track it down and having no success, they just palmed it off on Oscar and Carrie's new Server "Farm." And they were only too happy to have it.

Here's why it gets so convoluted. It turns out that the Chinese tech groups were well ahead of everyone in developing cell phones and service. They experimented in a lot of places. Tibet was close, isolated, tech starved and was easily manipulated by the Chinese government along with the cell company's research and development departments. They were soon hosting a texting service for a group of Tibetan monks spread throughout the mountainous countryside. Yeah, that's right, monks. The guys who live on mountain tops and don't talk and make B&B for little old ladies to drink. Well, they must do more than that. Apparently they have some very powerful backers with very deep pockets who want these guys to continue their good-deed-doing in perpetuity.......The monks do not know, nor care who is hosting their texting service as they have a sweetheart of a deal as long as Oscar and Carrie understand the program, (which they do).

There is some glitch in the monks' creed, constitution, preamble or bylaws that prohibit them from speaking. One of them, (a millennial I'm guessing) found that there was nothing mentioned about them communicating via text message with each other and quickly took advantage of that when he got them to sign a lease for a cell tower to be placed on their mountain. All the monks were given cell phones at the end of the deal and instead of tossing them or locking them up, they were dispensed to the monks, thinking they could be used as notepads, calculators or paperweights... When the Chinese cell phone operator found out what had happened, they just leased the "monk" business off. This must have fallen under the "Not my problem" clause, and taken care of after obscuring and obfuscating their dealings and the monks' identity.

So as it now stands, the monks are happy with their service, the finance company is busy consolidating and down sizing their departments and businesses, while Carrie and Oscar are happy with their built in revenue as well as the free money from their "severance" and are free to find other "renters" to grow their farming life.

As we drove back home that evening, we were happy and content in the thought that the "American way is alive and well" in the deep confines of rural Illinois.

Now Oscar is kept busy trying to figure out if anything is wrong with the system, while trying to learn to speak Tibetan.......... or is it Tibetionese?

Carrie is happy keeping the books, cashing the checks and tending to the baby. So much for farm life, huh?

CHAPTER 11

The Sausage King

*T*his one was a bit harder.

I had to turn the car around as we had all but passed it before Pat noticed and suggested that we might want to turn around and investigate this. There was no traffic as we were on Old Rte 66 in central Illinois. I-55 had taken the traffic from this road decades ago. I pulled the car off onto the shoulder and we looked through the windshield at the object of our scrutiny. I glanced at Pat and realized that we were both studying this pretty hard, trying to understand how we might find a story in it. It looked like just a bunch of crap laying under a sideless pole barn in the middle of a field......

The field looked overgrown with weeds, a little scrub brush and a couple of immature conifers that had started to grow up. It had been quite a few years since this place had anyone's attention for more than a minute. There was a gravel road, no, let's call it a path that ran about 50 feet straight up to the subject of our interest. Since there was no gate or signs, we decided to get a closer look. It was a brisk winter day in January and I was hesitant to leave the warmth of a perfectly good running car, but Pat was putting on her gloves and had already zipped her coat.

We were going in.

There was a chain link fence surrounding the place which we could not see from the road. Under the roof, we could see quite a few old rusted neon signs from a roadhouse, casino, restaurants and general store, what looked like coolers, a lot of them bent and pretty much useless stainless steel tables, stoves, and cabinets. The coolers and cabinets were either laying on their backs or propped up on their sides. The cabinets, randomly placed, were usually just set up on their ends with the doors open, laying on the ground or just hanging from one hinge. There was more than one nest from some critter making its home there. Buried under all of this was what looked to be an early 1960's black Lincoln Continental Convertible. We have a penchant for finding these don't you think? Anyway, back to the car. You know the one, suicide doors and looked to weigh in at about 6 tons. Think "Entourage". Nothing to get excited about, until I saw a rusty hole on the back left quarter panel by the tail light. As I looked closer I could see that it was riddled with bullet holes down both sides of it. Fairly large calibre bullet holes, and from the pattern, it looked like they were a spray from a machine gun. Hmmm.

After a brisk walk back to the car we decided on a plan. As usual, we found the closest town to this latest stash and went to get some lunch. Driving past the closed McDonalds and the still open Sonic, which we skipped and headed through town until, in a blink, we were through the town! I turned around in what used to be a strip center that may have had at least 3 generations of eateries in it in the past. Slowing down now as I drove through town the only thing I could think was that it must have died a very slow death.

There were some side streets that looked all but abandoned, as most of the houses had been torn down or burned down. I pulled down one of the side streets, parked and we got out to survey the lay of the land, so to speak.

You could tell the grid of what once was a residential area just by standing and looking straight across the overgrown yards from one barren street to the next. There was a hulk of an old school on the far north end. There were a few houses that looked still inhabitable, even though a boarded window here and there gave cause for re-evaluation, but, yes at least a few families were still holding out here, for what reason, I'll never know. Off to the south, a few RV's A few homes, more than a few blue tarps covering decaying who knows what underneath?

We were getting back in the car when a pickup truck came down the street. As he rolled his window down, I could see he was wearing a police uniform. He asked if he could help us so we gave a brief synopsis of our project and travels. This seemed to quench his inquisitive cop mind so I asked him about the pole barn just before you get into town. He looked us up and down again and was trying to decide if it was worthwhile telling this story, again. I thought I would sweeten the pot and asked if there was a place we could all go for lunch. He looked out of the windows, and then around the barren streets before he looked at us again and said, "Yeah, but not around here anymore." I said, "anything but Sonic" and he said, "we'll have to drive over to the Annex." Feeling safe enough, I told him we'd follow him.

We drove through town once again, but he turned left halfway through this coal starved city (thank you Harry Chapin) and we took a road that looked like it wouldn't really lead to anything for about a mile. Back around a few old back yard slag piles and in the distance, there was a group of trailers, some new construction and well, yes, it looked like an annex. There was a strip center anchored with a small grocery store on one end and a restaurant on the other. We pulled right next to the pickup that we were following and he led us into the "Country Inn".

The hostess welcomed us and Officer Bertram, or Bert as he preferred, as she seated us at a table. As she handed out the menus, I told her that Pat would be picking up the check…..didn't go over with the waitress or Pat, but Bert got a chuckle.

Since it was nice and comfortable in here without the stiff cold wind blowing dust in our faces, I thought I would explain in detail a bit more about our book and project. Bert seemed interested as I told about a couple of the stories that we had found so far. He stopped me when I mentioned the Red MGA Mark II Deluxe. He asked if Susan Meyers still owned it. Both Pat and I looked at each other and asked "How do you know Susan? " "I'll get to that. It'll be in this story," he said.

This was a "breakfast anytime" joint and so even though it was a bit after noon, we all decided on the Farmers Brunch: sausage, eggs, hash browns, bacon, corned beef hash and toast. Coffee all around Bert said, as this was going to take a while.

Bert's story telling included waving a fork around with a piece of food on it to make a point before he shoveled it in his already full mouth to continue talking. Jeez, what a mess. I don't know how we made it through that. Apparently Bert wasn't married or had missed that class on etiquette in cop school.

"Well, getting back to the story of the *stuff under the pole barn*", Bert began;

"Melvin Fitzmeyer was the son of a European farmer who settled here in southern Illinois in the late 1800's after his family had immigrated to Pennsylvania in the 1700's. Melvin's farm began producing pork for the area and through the next two generations had grown to be one of the greater producers of pork in the Midwest. By the time prohibition had started as well as the depression, Melvin and his family were well insulated from the problems of most folk around here."

"This is where the story gets twisted though. It seemed that the family had this "un-written codicil" that required the parents of each future generation to name the first born male Melvin, as a memorial to their late ancestor that brought them here. Now this Melvin, who took over the great Pork Empire from his father Melvin soon became known as Mel "The Sausage King" due to his increased advertising and promotions of the products in the mid 1930's. You know, radio jingles, contests and company sponsored picnics and church socials, all featuring some of the pork products the Mel the Sausage King was pushing at that particular time. The Sausage King had a son, after his 5th try (all girls up to that point) his son Mel was born in 1945. So from this point on we will refer to "Mel the Sausage King" and "Mel the Lesser", his less than useless son.

If you have not gathered this, Illinois is pretty flat all told and just as boring if you are driving from one end of it to the other. I personally learned this at a fairly young age. On one of my family's summer sojourns to a midwestern college, and this one was probably the University of Minnesota, I found myself contemplating just how boring it was. I sat in the backseat of an fairly new Chevy Sedan looking out of one of the back windows. We must have been on old Rt. 66 before it had been turned into the double nickel or Interstate 55. We began to slow down. The sky had been getting darker as a late summer storm began to form over the plaines. The car had pulled over and come to a complete stop as all of the other cars had started to do. I was picked up from the back seat and brought to a crowd of people who had formed and they were all pretty excited. Now, this part is all from my parents repeating this story over the years. Being a kid, I wasn't really into situational awareness at that time, so whatever was going on, I accepted it. The fact is, there was a fairly large tornado that had formed in the flatness of these Illinois Praries and on Highway 66 we all stood safely watching it slowly meandering back and forth destroying the countryside at will. My memory now is that it was just like the tornado on the Wizard of Oz. I probably didn't realize until much later that those small black twisting pieces of whatever, were indeed, roofs, doors, cows, chickens and various other pieces of farm stuff. Probably the entire contents of a barn or two. Maybe that's where the seed for this book was planted. So once again, I am sure that Hollywood has formed my memory of what really was or what may have been. Either way, I still remember it being a very scary time, even as I was held, safe in my fathers arms.

So this was not my only experience with tornados. It turns out that the historic 1959 tornado that did so much damage in St. Louis and had bounced it's way Northeast and touched down on Westhues Way and proceeded to take out a 100 year old ak tree in our front yard.

The story on that one was that it happened before any of the warning systems were out so that it happened in an instant and in another instant, it was gone. The tree fell nicely between the two houses on Westhues Way such that there was minimal damage. Oh, yes, I slept through it since in 1959 I was almost 7 years old. There was plenty of activity on our street from hearing that story so many times so I got the reputation of being able to sleep through anything that was thrown my way.

Now, back to "Mel the Sausage king and Mel the lessor":

"By this time the family owned a series of hog farms around the state as well as their own meat processing plant in Centralia known as Central States Meat Products. Through the generations of hard work the family had been rewarded with wealth and prosperity. When The Sausage King's son came into the picture, he wasn't really interested in building wealth as much as spending wealth. You know, lots of fast cars, which wound up as wrecked cars soon enough. The kid just wasn't that coordinated and daddy would always buy a new one. There were a couple of brushes with the law, back when I was still in the academy," Bert added. "Most were minor scrapes, you know, minor assaults pleaded down to disturbing the peace. "

"After high school Mel got into motorcycles and in his twenties was known for selling weed here and there. There was suspicion of coke in the 70's but nothing was ever proved."

"Mel talked his father into fronting a restaurant which was just a front for a nightclub for him to run called "The Hide Away." Remains of the place could just be made out, if you looked, at the beginning of town just when you come in. Just an empty strip center now. Mel's father built that whole development for him to manage, but he was too interested in the bar as it turned out."

"By this time, Mel was running with a pretty mean biker crowd. Lots of drugs, prostitution, assaults, thieving, stolen vehicles, break-ins….. you name it and it was happening. That was about the time I came on the force. We had about 12,000 people in town here but we needed a lot more law enforcement than our full time sheriff's station staff of 30 officers could provide."

"That car that you saw under the pole barns outside of town was part of this mess. No one ever saw what happened to that Lincoln, but there were many unsubstantiated rumors. They sort of confirmed that at one party Mel threw for his group which included some major debauchery, he got mad, for no particular reason and took it out on his brand new car. He pulled out an automatic Kalashnikov, you know, an AK-47, and let it have it. Both sides. All four tires. He destroyed the front grill and engine. The next morning he had no idea what had happened and was ready to kill, until one of his toadies explained it to him so that even he couldn't deny it. It was then hidden away out on the old Danvers Farm with a bunch of crap from one of his failed bars. Keith Danvers said that he might charge admission to see it if he ever gets enough interest in this town's story. I seriously doubt that will ever occur."

"There were always plenty of bikers coming and going around here, we had four motels and six bars, all owned by Mel the Lesser at this time. Mel also opened up a chrome shop for his buddies in the motorcycle clubs. He always had a bunch of people coming and going there. Got pretty suspicious. We saw he had plenty of what you might call, the wrong types of people coming over there, as our surveillance details picked up. We tried to figure out just what was going on, but we rarely caught anyone with anything big, I mean some dime bags, a few joints and a couple bags of coke every now and then, but considering the amount of other crimes, and sheer volume of malcontents and trouble makers coming through here, the small amount of drugs just didn't add up to the large amount of trouble that they were causing around here. The crime statistics that we submitted to the state raised some eyebrows."

"About then, we had heard from the FBI out of Indianapolis about some missing persons. Not the runaway kids, or a spouse who skipped out on her old man, but heavy hitters that were into some pretty dirty dealings. The trail dead-ended here. Then the FBI from St. Louis and KC came over. When the Chicago authorities got involved the Feds figured we better pull all the agencies together for an official pow-wow."

"This was now well into the 1980's. The investigation continued over 5 years with leaps and starts and plenty of setbacks along the way, but when 1986 came it was the beginning of the end, as well as the beginning of the end of the town also. You see, almost half of the town was employed in some way by Central States Meat Processing, you know, Mel The Sausage King? They weren't involved in any crimes, and nothing could be pinned on The Sausage King, but the kid, now that was a different story."

"When The Sausage King was on top of the heap and his son was being groomed for taking over this empire, it seems Mel the Lesser had different thoughts. As I said, his biker friends had some connections with some very bad people and it turned out that they needed to get rid of a body.

Mel kidded that they could drop it off at one of the hog lots and it would be gone in a matter of minutes. Up until this point, no one besides his own lackeys and toadies had ever taken Mel the Lesser seriously. All they had to do was shave the head and pull the teeth. Mel knew that from tossing the neighborhood cats into the hog pens when he was younger. He got caught and punished by The Sausage King. "The Lesser" figured out what got him caught and vowed never to do it again (get caught)."

"It was easy enough to instruct his crew how to get rid of hair and teeth, but it turned out that they were just putting the teeth in the empty jars from the Vienna Sausages that Mel the Lesser went through like candy. And bags and bags of hair.........One informant told us that they had an entire shelf full of these little jars before Mel had a brain storm, and he had the solution.

Nitric acid was the solution. He built a chrome shop on the outskirts of town. A vat of hot nitric acid is a handy thing to have around when you need to dispose of things….fast. His crowd was always chroming one thing or another on their bikes and so it seemed pretty popular. So now with a chrome shop, he had no problem getting rid of the hair and teeth, also the occasional cat." "I'm telling you Mel was not only a badass, he was a dick too!" said Bert. "Mel was running a gruesome little business here in town."

"When The Sausage King died in 1984, his funeral was well attended. The feds also noted many people whose circle Mel The Sausage King, would just not have included. Nothing was ever traced back to him, but the kid…..his more nefarious reasons for owning the chrome shop and hog farms became very obvious during the course of the investigation."

"The Feds found that people were bringing bodies from as far away as the east coast and as far west as Denver. Most of the people were alive when they were brought out here. Just tricked into a "roadtrip". They were kept well lubed with liquor and drugs so they never really had any idea they had pissed off somebody bad until the very end. "

"Some people that testified at the trial said that one guy was told exactly what was going to happen to him on the way out. Apparently he knew about it for the 3 hour ride back here from wherever they found him. Somewhere down in Little Egypt. Apparently a hit carried out by one of Mel's biker friends, but no evidence or body and with all the other stuff, there was just nothing to go on so we dropped it. It was still very horrible. "

"That was how I knew about Susan Meyers. She showed up for the trial. It turns out that guy that was told what was going to happen to him, Scott something…..He called himself a doctor. Yeah, right, Doctor of the Con. He had a friend who would print up whatever identity that he might need, false name, drivers license, medical license, dental license, you name it, you could be it. When they were digging through his past, I think he started out as some sort of computer whiz back in the old Univac days. Ms. Meyers had some connection to him, an old boyfriend if I were to guess. She didn't say much, but she had some interest in the whereabouts of this Scott character. I can't rightly say whether she was pleased or annoyed with the outcome upon her finding out his final disposition." Bert stared off into the distance and pondered that last thought for a moment.

"When The Feds were at their height in town here, there must have been at least 20 to 30 of them. One crew that was auditing the chrome shop's books had found that the amount of nitric acid that they were purchasing was nowhere near what was needed for the volume of chrome that they were processing. The audit also showed that the hundreds of thousands of dollars that were listed as chrome work did not match the amount of chrome, nickel and copper materials that were being purchased. That's how they broke the case. Then it just all collapsed like a house of cards. The EPA also got involved, as apparently they were just dumping the exhausted nitric acid in the local slag pile runoff ponds, if you can call them that. Caused all sorts of havoc with the Environmental and Conservation Departments. I mean, you look at all of that mess, caused by someone else decades ago. How in the hell do they think a few more gallons of that crap would make a rat's ass of a difference?" More staring into the distance and pondering by Bert; "They all wanted a piece and got it."

"All the friends Mel had turned their backs on him. He didn't have much family left and his sisters certainly didn't want anything to do with him. The sisters were left in charge of the pork business. I don't know which one of them is the Sausage King now." Bert chuckled at his own joke.

"Mel the Lesser sold off his business assets one by one but he never could get his hands on what was left of his family's empire. Piece by piece his properties were all sold to pay for his high priced lawyers.

At first he was providing legal counsel for all of his low life friends, but in the end, all he had left went to his own defense."

"Most of the townspeople who worked for the family, they didn't want anything to do with the town or the blighted history anymore and started to move away. It turns out that a nasty rumor ran amuck that a lot of the bodies were ground up and used as fertilizer on the yards in town. This was the landscaping company that was of course run by Mel. No truth could ever be found of that, but that didn't keep damn near the whole town from up and moving. Those that could, left for parts unknown, those who had some money bought into the new Annex that you are in right now. Still the same town and people, but just moved far enough over to keep the stench of the Sausage King from drifting over the slag piles."

"As the investigation turned up, more than 100 missing people were connected to Mel and his enterprise. The FBI from St. Louis, Chicago, Kansas City and Indianapolis all found ties to at least one of their cases to this little slice of heaven here. At the height of the trial there were enough people coming in here each day that the airport had to start a shuttle service just for the Feds. I understand that they paid dearly for that as the no-bid contract with unlimited scope brought in almost another half a million dollars to the airport commission. Soon there was an investigation of the airport commission, but the money trail here was so convoluted that they decided to just focus on Mel as they could all agree to point their fingers at him and not themselves. There was even a contingent from the Hoffa investigation, but that never panned out. It is rumored that up to two hundred more could have met their ends here, but the Feds couldn't find any more solid evidence. They may open it up if they get some more substantial evidence." Bert said that he sure hates that those people cannot get closure.

As brunch was quickly heading to dinner time and Bert had that hungry look in his eye when he looked toward the rotating dessert carousel, we thanked him for his time and took his number in case any questions might come up later. We said our goodbyes and headed for the car for the drive home. We both made a mental note to contact Susan about some unanswered questions when we got home.

After we got home, we decided to forget about calling Susan.

CHAPTER 12

The Tour Bus and Max

*O*n one of the rare instances that I was traveling alone, I pulled into a very nice compound with a beautiful tree-lined road coming up from the state highway and delivering me right to the circular drive in front of the house.

Max met me as he walked down the steps when I pulled up, right on time. Now this was a house! And it really didn't need a barn. I mean you could park a couple of tractors in the living room alone! I don't know if this really was a farm or not, but when the owner invited me up to see the bus he said that it was still stored in his barn. Who am I to judge…..

Max, it turns out, was an old rocker who played the 1960's and 1970's state fair and theatre circuits around the USA traveling by tour bus. Originally a classically trained trombonist, he heard the calling in high school and like all true musicians, set off in a panel van with some of his friends to make their mark on the music industry here in the states. Max is in his 70's right now and a bit slower, in movement only, but still actively involved in the "business."

We hit it off immediately and both instantly knew that we were meant to be friends. Max was a singer with a group that had a brief brush with fame in the mid 70's with a pop hit. Max was the singer on the record and rode that hit as his ticket to become a well respected music producer around the midwest and especially Nashville in the 80's and 90's. When you see his face pop up on the internet today, you still see the straight arrow gentleman who forged ahead when the band and their one hit that could not be recreated. Max has even been teaching himself to play organ again with a recently acquired 'Baby B3", a 1954 Hammond M3 organ that he practices everyday.

I learned all of this about Max as we had a cup of coffee in the kitchen on this sunny afternoon in rural Madison County Illinois. Max and his lovely wife Mary have been living on this "hobby" farm for the last 20 years with the idea that they would retire here and raise Westie's. They have two of them right now. Two of the cutest, most stubbornly independent balls of white fur you would ever want to be ignored by. Well, they are still going strong, Max and Mary, that is. Neither have retired yet and I don't see it happening any time soon.

Max suggested that we take a walk down to the barn, which meant that he would drive us down in his custom combination golf cart, yard tractor and salt spreader during the winter months. When we got to the barn, it looked like something out of the Anheuser Busch family compound. Not really a barn, as it had polished concrete floors that you would swear were marble. It looked like a barn on the outside, but inside, WOW! The upper floors were all open in the center to see the exposed roof trusses all natural red oak. There were walkways and other rooms on the first and second loft level.

This was truly the man cave that Max had always wanted. A large music studio was on one side, which was completely soundproof to the rest of the building. His office filled another complete corner of the second level, allowing him a total view of everything going on in the studio and control room, as well as a sweeping view of the valley outside leading up to their home. Oh yeah, a two-person elevator to get you between floors was available if you were not up to climbing the ornately carved walnut staircase with a raging hand carved, red oak stallion at both ends. Nice touch.

Max gave me the full nickel tour. It was amazing. And after the tour of this facility that would easily compete with any commercial sound stage, Max opened a door, flipped on a light switch and here we stood in front of a beaten down, road weary, 1954 GMC PD 5501 Scenic Cruiser.

It was big, and as buses go, pretty ugly. It was smelly as it apparently had been marking its territory by leaking oil, hydraulic fluid and diesel fuel as a protest for being taken off the road for the last hundred or so years, but, when I turned to say so, I saw Max with one of the biggest smiles I have ever seen on the face of any man. No doubt, this was his baby. It stands proud amongst his most cherished accomplishments.

I was introduced to Max by a friend of mine, also another musician/producer whom I had been playing keyboards for as a hired gun in the STL area for the past few years. When Paul heard I was writing this collection of stories, he called and insisted that I needed to meet Max. Paul made the introduction via email and left us to our own. Paul could tell two kindred souls when he saw them.

A few emails back and forth and here we were. I wanted to know about the bus as this was technically a "barn story".

Max pushed a button and the door to the bus magically opened and he motioned me to climb up the first couple of steps, to the driver's area. I could see back aways and there were clearly 8 first class seats on this level as well as a kitchenette. Burgundy leather seats with white piping. Each seat had an adjustable foot rest and each seat would be remotely adjustable to fit the contours of any musician, large or small, male or female. Behind those were three more steps up to the scenic cruiser area which had been heavily modified as Max told me, including a restroom with a shower and one large sleeping area for the "star". There was also a small dining area that doubled as a practice area when the seats and table were stowed away. All the comforts of home as required by the band. Max showed me his seat and said that his seat had allowed him to criss cross the country many times during his touring days.

The bus had a very special place in his heart. He cut his eye teeth with the music industry here. Even as a side man and star singer on the hit single, he was not one to let grass grow under his feet. Soon to leave the band, he went off on his own to manage bands such as Spanky and Our Gang through his record label, American Eagle Recordings and his agency Million Dollar artists. Max started and operated quite a few businesses and he became very successful in all, however that burgundy leather bus seat was always where he sought his solace.

So off he went on a decade long search for this bus. It led him to GM in Detroit, home of the manufacturer of the bus, then down to

Dallas to Greyhound's headquarters and through a number of private owners until he finally located just that bus in a storage yard close to Indianapolis.

Max, no stranger to making deals, finally found his "baby" and negotiated the purchase of this vehicle and the transportation of it back to his "farm" for $4500! Apparently Max had a gift.

I spent many hours listening to Max and his stories about the road, his life, his good times and his not so good times. How his eyes would light up as he spoke about his life. All through it, however, he still kept that smile on his face. There are a few people that strike me the way Max did. I describe it as having that certain "twinkle" in his eye when you catch him in a sideways glance. There is a sort of mischievousness, just looking to get out, and anyone who says different is itchin' for a fight.

So now we stand in front of it again and Max has assured me that it does run and that when it is finally restored to his specifications, that I will get in on the second Maiden Voyage of this continental vehicle.

I forgot to ask Max if he has his CDL! If not, I think I know a guy that can print up a couple for us......

CHAPTER 13

The Biplane As a Getaway Vehicle

We spotted what might be the remains of a very old biplane off to the side of a long driveway. At one time it looked like it may have been part of a display that could have been mounted on a pole or raised up somehow to catch your attention. Now this was a down right invitation to drive up and ask some questions. I mean if they wanted privacy, they surely would have removed this relic by now.

I turned into the driveway and stopped to look at this historical piece of aviation left rotting in a pile of stone, rocks and iron. It was a biplane, and from what I recall it may have well been a Jenny, much like my Uncle Paul's first plane that he bought sometime in the 1930's after borrowing money from his two younger brothers, my Uncle Larry and my dad Art. It was just bits and pieces of a frame. The fabric had long been torn away. The cockpit could just be identified by some leather that had been wrapped around the cockpit to ease sliding in and getting out of the plane. The stick was gone and the floorboards had rotted away. There were pieces of the instrument panel with just a few holes that might identify it as such. A few control cables lay strewn about, I'm sure most of them had long ago been scavenged to give their lives so that another farm project might stay viable for a little longer.

It was a dreary fall day with a light drizzle of rain. Much like this plane may have seen if it were in battle over Verdun, or the Somme, or maybe just as a reconnaissance plane reporting on German troop movement in the trenches a couple of hundred feet below.

Ok, I went away for a little bit, but I'm back now. Pat was already back sitting in the car trying to stay warm and dry. We could see activity up at the farmhouse and near the old barn. The few outbuildings on this place were well maintained and painted. I got back in the truck and we headed up towards the main house.

This was a typical two story farmhouse we have seen all over Illinois. It was sided in horizontal white clapboard, with green accents on shutters on each side of every window. The house was up on a small hill, so the shutters were sure to be functional as the winds rolling down the Illinois prairie can get quite fierce. There were no dormers attached to this house, but an addition was added to it on the left side, and in keeping with the style, continued the porch around back to the front. The front porch had its own roof for protection and was supported with four equally spaced support columns. There was a rail with hand-turned spindles between each column except where the three stairs came up from the yard in the very center of the porch. There, the rails from the columns ran down the stairs terminating in the ground and forming a nice little entryway with a sign between them at the top. On it were the hand-painted, carved words

"Bienvenue, Mon Ami's".

As I admired the historical significance of the carving, the owner came down and asked: "Like it?" Always aware of someone trying to trick me into buying something I had no need of, I asked if it was original, to which the reply was "Of course" and the disclaimer that, well, his father actually added the apostrophe and "s" to it decades ago. It seems he thought that the American plural of the French word for friend (ami) should be ami's and thus added it. It was a good job I admit, you could not tell it wasn't the original unless the original French owner was an illiterate, but I kept my mouth shut as I had often been told.

Robert Gross introduced himself to Pat and me, while wiping his hands on a blue bandana recently plucked from his back pocket. He said "just call me Reg". He offered his hand as an introduction and we shook as he ushered us up the stairs so we could stand under the dry porch overhang. I started my "farmyard pitch", as the "elevator pitch" just never did sound right out here. He interrupted me towards the end and called into the house for his wife, Maureen, who came out after putting her bread in the oven. He wanted her to hear it, so I started over again. When I pointed to the pile of parts that used to be an airplane, they glanced at each other and then back to Pat and me to sum us up. It must not have taken too long, because they both started talking in agreement that this was a nice story that they would like to share. Since this was going to take some time, I asked if they would like us to come back later at a more convenient time, again, they both agreed that now was just fine. This weather would keep him out of the fields for a day or so and everything else could wait. I walked back to the car to get our notebooks. We long ago learned not to approach a farmer with a notepad, computer or briefcase, because doing so would immediately cause suspicion that would take awhile to break down if ever. No, just casually dressed travelers, maybe looking for directions was always the best approach.

Maureen invited us into the house to sit in the kitchen while she finished her baking. Now this was a great welcome.

A brief aside about what we have learned so far: Sitting on the porch and talking, you really had to sell. Being invited to the parlor to talk was very formal and you could never determine your position with them. However, an invite to sit in the kitchen? We were accepted like family. Iced tea all around and some shortbread cookies were offered and accepted. Now at this point, Pat and I had met quite a few southern Illinois farmers and other locals and we had both formed our opinions fairly quickly with some and not so quickly with some others. Robert and Maureen were certainly genuine, friendly people who could sit and talk with anyone. We had a quick tour of their home and since it was raining we took a chance and skipped the barn, outbuildings and property tour. No, we already had found our story and settled back in the kitchen to hear them both tell it.

Robert, or Reg as he said to call him, was the fifth generation on this property. It had grown from his great, great, great, grandfather Emil Gross who migrated from Thun Switzerland in 1874. Another case of wanderlust and the draw of new adventure in a new world. Emil and his wife had their farm and raised a family. Their son Charles and his wife Charlotte had a daughter Maryann who was born in June of 1900. Maryann had a beau from the area named Mike Joplin. Maryann and Mike had planned to get married as Mike signed up for the army in 1917. Both sets of parents refused to allow them to get married under these circumstances and so Mike went to fight in the Great War under the flag of France in the LaFayette Escadrille.

He was killed in action in 1917. His body was sent back home for burial with the honor of the French Combatants Cross.

Maryann did not recover from that experience for a long time. She fell into a deep depression, although in those days it was called "in one of her moods". Although she still did her chores and helped with everything else around the farm, she always retreated to her room after dinner and after mass on Sunday at St. Mark's Catholic Church. As she grew through her 20's and into her thirties, she gradually grew back into the family and also the community.

In 1934 an airshow came to town for a week's visit.. To get the word out, the pilots would take off in every direction and "buzz" the neighboring farms, fields and towns, occasionally dropping pamphlets into the larger gatherings of onlookers. One such farm they buzzed was the Emil Gross Farm. Yes, everyone came out to see the planes and you could even see some of the other brightly painted birds flying their mission over other farms on every horizon they turned to. This story was passed down on this point alone: This was the first time Maryann had laughed and smiled in over a decade. It's almost as if the world had instantly gone from being black and white to Technicolor! Her smile was like that. She could brighten up the day for anyone when she smiled. The whole household noticed it and although no one outright would point it out, but that smile was so contagious that everyone around her would catch it when she was heading their way.

She took the farm truck to the air field the next day and found out about the show. Two shows a day, 12 planes in all. Stunts, Acrobatics, Re-enacted WWI battles. The field was filled with airplanes. Most all of them were the biplanes, or the popular Jennys from World War I. And parts! If you didn't know it, you would soon learn that it takes LOTS of spare parts, both new and used to keep these machines in the air. There was a carnival atmosphere in the air. People were running to get anywhere, most though, ran to the bleachers so they could have a nice seat within earshot of the announcer, "Barker" as they were called, and not be drowned out by the noise of the engines, constantly starting and stopping. Revving up, backfiring, and sometimes catching on fire! The most dangerous occurrence for a pilot. The most cherished times for any pilot was when they were in the air. The most terrifying nightmare was of crashing and being trapped, alive and conscious with 25 gallons of highly volatile gasoline about to explode above you and you were trapped, about to be......

Rides and FLYING LESSONS! They were setting up tents around the airfield. Some small, some larger to keep the crowds interested and inside out of the weather in the case of rain. Some tents were to house the mechanics and the planes which needed constant attention. Uh, the planes needed the constant attention. The mechanics all pretty much kept to themselves. There were even trucks with spare planes! There was a set of bleachers set up facing the runway. They hired crews to work from around the community. Sheriff Franklin was there, everyone called him "Tank" as he was a decorated tank commander in the Great War. He and his deputy Steven Neidermeyer, who noticed Maryann immediately, were checking permits and flying certificates of all the pilots. Deputy Neidermeyer tipped his hat to her as he walked past her looking for some more certificates to verify. Steven Neidermeyer had known Maryann all of their lives. They went to school together and he even talked about joining the Escadrille with Mike, but for whatever reason, stayed back as a constable. Although a constable's job was not really essential back then and he was given an exemption by the local draft board that his uncle, Torbeck Neidermeyer, the bank president, was in charge of. Getting his nephew deferred and foreclosing on widows and orphans was his legacy. No, Maryann was never interested in Steven for those reasons alone.

As she walked around looking at each plane and watching the pilots and mechanics working on them, she noticed how they all were working very closely together, as a team. Pilots handing tools to mechanics, mechanics standing on a step talking and gesturing to the pilots. Some doing a somewhat awkward ballet in trying to start the engines; the starter yelling "Ignition", the pilot returning with the call of "Contact", and the mechanic reaching his arms up to the propellor, kicking his right foot and leg out before straining with all his might to pull the prop down and around before quickly ducking out of the way so he wouldn't become ground beef.

This was just the set up and "rehearsal' day before the real thing hit over the weekend. Continuing her stroll down the flight line, she saw one lone plane sitting at the end of the line. No one was working on it or even near it. It had the pilot's name "Irish O'Toole" painted on both sides of the cockpit, but neither a pilot nor mechanic was around this plane. She looked around and saw a tall man in dirty canvas coveralls standing by a truck, smoking a cigarette. He had an 8 panel newsboy hat pulled down over his forehead, while his red hair stuck out from under it. He stood so that she could only see his profile, his head tilted down with his left hand cupping the cigarette. He would glance at her between drags. She pretended not to notice and kept walking around the plane. He flicked the ember from the butt and pressed it out with his foot. He then field stripped the cigarette until there was nothing left of it. He started walking over to what Maryann was certain was his plane.

"Nice plane" she said, "is it yours?" He replied quietly that it was his. He was waiting on a mechanic to come back from town with a part for his carburetor. Something about it cutting out over fifteen hundred feet, whatever that meant. Things being what they were, even a shy man must eat once a day and since he didn't really have any prospects for a meal until his plane was repaired, he decided to try and make small talk. He didn't have a chance. As soon as he looked up she was a fountain of questions of just about everything that she saw on the plane. Her long lost beau was shot down over France in LaFayette Escadrille, she started, and that's all she had to say.

It seems that "Irish's" shyness and Maryann's depression had both disappeared as soon as they saw each other. They spent the afternoon standing around or sitting under the wing of his Jenny discussing the plane, the show, the war.......everything but their past. Both had realized this well into the afternoon but neither had the experience nor inclination to try and explore further. When the sun was hanging a bit lower in the sky and the shadows were beginning to get longer, Maryann got up and extended her hand to thank Irish for his time and an interesting afternoon. She looked around and saw that things had all but closed down while they were invested in their talk.

"Is one of these tents the cafeteria?" she asked. "No," he replied, "everyone's on their own for room and board. I just usually sleep in my plane." he said. "Well what about dinner?" she asked. Irish said he had some hard rolls and a bottle of ale in the plane. When she heard that she grabbed him by the arm and said, "There is no way I will let a brave hero of the Great War sleep and eat in his old plane, no matter how close he might be to it. You will just come home with me and have dinner with us."

Irish thought things were looking up. Maryann certainly was...into his eyes. "I have the truck right over there," she pointed. "We'll just go on back to the farm. We'll have a good dinner and I know that my family would just love having you stay with us. It's settled then" she said, somewhat uncharacteristically, as they walked to the flatbed and settled in for the drive to the farm.

When they arrived this Thursday late afternoon, the farm was still abuzz with activity and Maryann walked Irish up the steps as more than a few of her brothers' eyes were upon them. She saw her father just coming out of the barn and waved him over to "meet an honest to goodness War Hero!" By this time her mother had come out of the house and two of her brothers started over to see what was going on before her father admonished them to get back to work. Removing his gloves and slapping them on his leg to knock the dust off of them, he reached his hand out and said, "It's an honor to meet you sir. Where did you see action?"

"I mostly flew as a trainer for the new pilots. I bounced around a few different outfits before we were involved in the Battle of Amiens. I flew for the British in that one."

This was all the old man needed and when Maryann said that she had invited him to stay with them, well, he would have it no other way. A fine dinner was had that Thursday evening and the whole family stayed up late to listen to Irish and his stories of the war.

The next morning, Maryann took him back to the airfield that was just beginning to wake up. The parts for his plane had been delivered and were sitting in the cockpit, along with a bill for fuel. Maryann recognized the invoice and before he even saw it, she grabbed it and tucked it away in her pocket. It was already planned that she would be back to watch the Friday afternoon show and bring him back to the house around 6 pm. On her way back to the farm, she stopped by the Barstow Farm and Fuel Supply to drop off his invoice and tell them to cover it on the Emil Gross Farm Account. "And any other that comes up from Irish O'Toole's plane."

She felt certain that her father would agree. She was right.

She was right on time for the show and paid her fifty cents to sit in the grandstand. Upon noticing that most people were there with their families or brother and sisters or mother and fathers with their children in tow, Maryann felt quite old now. She was thinking back on her missed youth and maybe how silly she looked at almost 35, watching a young man like a high school girl watches her crush play baseball.

Then the planes started, taxied a bit and then began taking off, sometimes two and three abreast! They climbed gracefully, turned, rolled, side slipped, spun, dove, stalled and any of the other terms the announcer may have called out during the show. This was exciting, and as she was watching the planes, trying to figure out which one Irish was piloting, she felt a hand on her shoulder as Irish settled down next to her in the bleachers. He was dirty again and smelled like gasoline. "The carburetor is still leaking. I'm lucky I didn't burn up alive on that first test flight today. I've been working on it all day and just can't get it to stop. I think it may have warped the throttle body when the last mechanic put it on. I knew I should have done it myself" he said as he slapped his knee with his hand.

Well, it was over for today and they drove back to the farm. When her father Charles asked him about the carburetor, Irish explained that nothing from the Farm and Fuel Supply would work as this was a special side draft carburetor for the Curtiss OX-5 Engine. Charles said, "Well, I know a fella down on the Kaskaskia River that has one of those OX-5 engines that he *says* he bought war surplus and put on a boat that he races on the river every so often. Why don't you give me the old one and I'll take it over to Jimmie's tomorrow and see if he can fix it or replace it."

Well, it meant missing the rest of the air show, but not the worst thing that could happen to both of them.

The Flying Show folded up their tents and headed to Des Moines Iowa for the next show. Maryann and the family decided it would be best to pull the plane down the road and put it in their barn until the carburetor came back. And come back it did, although not right away.

It seems Jimmie was having problems with his wife and she was really tired of him spending all the family's money on that damn boat, he told Maryann's father to "make him an offer for the entire shootin' match."

So The Gross Farm now had not only an airplane in it's barn but a racing boat as well. Now this all had taken place over the course of a couple of weeks, and Maryann and Irish were seen pretty much everywhere together. Some bad weather had set in and because the fields were plowed and muddy, there was no way for the plane to take off. Irish earned his keep by working on the farm for room and board. It also didn't hurt that he and Maryann had become extremely fond of one another. As the summer turned into fall everyone was talking about Irish hanging around and working the farm until the next summer when he could catch up with the flying troupe again. Not a bad idea. Until Sheriff Tank Franklin showed up and asked to see "that flyer feller you are boarding".

Sheriff Franklin had some questions about the validity of the certificate that Irish had shown him last summer. The questioning went alright as questionings went, but everyone including Maryann soon had some kind of doubt as to who Irish was. All of the certificates and documents that Irish had looked valid and satisfied any question as to who he was. There was however this one lingering problem. There had been a bank robbery in Minnesota a few years back. The investigation of the getaway car went dead at the field where the Flying Show had been the week before. The G-men were on this and had followed every lead as best they could. They were looking at flying certificates. It seems that Patrick O'Riley was a pilot. Had a Jenny, flew in WWI, flew in a few flying circuses and air races around the Midwest, but could never be found. The investigation had been expanded to include any variation of the name as well. Someone pointed out that the name O'Riley could be easily changed and that any Irish name with an "O apostrophe" should be investigated.

The next week everyone seemed to know about this and of course Irish O'Toole was on the tip of everyone's tongues. Maryann and her entire family tried to smother these little fires everywhere they popped up. And they did pop up. One story even had Maryann worried. There was a blue Jenny involved in the "bombing" of a gambling joint called the Shady Rest down on Rt. 13 near Crab Orchard. She drove down there one day and found a whole nest of undesirables she would have rather NOT have heard about. In 1926 the "Shelton Gang" and the "Birger Gang" were resolving their many differences with a feud, much like the Hatfield and McCoys, only Much, Much more blood. One iteration of a story that she had heard from a banker from Shawneetown was that there were two pilots and one blue Jenny that tried to drop some homemade bombs on the Shady Rest that was owned by someone lacking in any Moral compass named Charlie Birger. After hearing only parts of the story, Maryann decided she wanted to drop her investigation immediately after saying good afternoon.

Now there were hundreds of Jennys flying around America after the Great War. And there were many people flying them. There were many support staff and there were TOO many unsavory sorts woven in with them, as she was finding out. There were too many. She would rather trust in the man she was falling in love with, the man that she knew and not let her mind be clouded by the back road myths she seemed to be collecting.

The Sheriff had been by a few more times and taken more and more information and asked more and more questions, to no avail. He said that the G-men were coming in next week. The next day Deputy Neidermeyer told Maryann that Tank had alerted the Feds that he, in all probability, had driven the suspect to ground, on the Emil Gross Farm.

Over the next few days, the farm never seemed to be without an investigator from either the local police, county police, special investigators and/or the Illinois State Police knocking at the door. They had all been satisfied, after first looking in the barn and verifying that the plane was still there, that Irish was off on a trip to scavenge parts for his plane.

In the days before the Feds were to show up, Sheriff Tank Franklin and Deputy Steve Neidermeyer had started taking turns sitting in their car watching the house for any suspicious signs. They saw nothing other than local farm chores, nothing was out of step. The Deputy glared at the Barstow Farm and Fuel Supply Company truck as it passed by him even as the driver, who was a friend of his son, Douglas, waved to him. The truck pulled around the back of the house to drop off some crates of parts for a "brand new, state of the art, thermostatically and environmentally controlled chicken coop". When the truck left and a few hours had passed, Maryann and her father walked out to look at the crates with the Deputy who had now become interested in it also. Not usually a man to swear, Charles began a list of profanities that would make a sailor blush. Picking up pieces and throwing them down as he kicked up a cloud a dirt, Steven slowly figured out that "that stupid son of a bitch from the Farm and Fuel Supply had delivered the wrong parts! He didn't order this and was "sure as hell not going to pay for it OR its shipping" to straighten this mess out. Maryann got the invoice from the house and convinced her father that it was just the one crate that did not belong and that the rest of the order was indeed what they had ordered.

"First that damn telephone that I didn't want and now this!"

He of course was referring to the wire strung overhead from branches of their trees from the main road all the way up to the house to a device he didn't understand, want or need. Maryann said, "I'll show you. I'll call into town and have them bring the right crate."

All seemed to settle down and Niedermeyer went back to his car. About 10 PM the deputy was relieved by the sheriff who would sit there until morning. Neidermeyer was promptly there at 8 PM to relieve the sheriff and took his post watching the house and buildings. The farm compound had been its usual flurry of morning activity so far and today was no different.

At 10 PM the Farm Supply truck showed up with the correct crate to exchange for the incorrect crate, and if Neidermeyer had been paying attention, he would have seen that the crate in question had already been opened and resealed with nails through some splintered wood. He would have also seen Maryann touch the crate as it was gently placed on the Barstow Farm and Fuel Supply flatbed. He should have also noticed Maryann waving to the flatbed as it turned onto the state road and disappeared, leaving a cloud of blue smoke in its path. Just as soon, the sheriff's car and a black sedan emerged from the cloud of blue smoke and turned into the driveway. Tank and his new entourage got out and immediately tried to serve an arrest warrant for Patrick Irish O'Riley. Charles and Maryann Gross quickly shook their heads and quizzically looked at the head Fed. "I'm sorry sir, but, like we have told the sheriff and deputy, we haven't seen him now for, what...maybe a good week. You are welcome to look around." The words had hardly hit the ground when another group of cars pulled up into the yard. Troops of State Police poured out and took up stations all around the farm. Maryann saw that they were even at another group of outbuildings a couple of fields over but still their property. She said that she didn't think that the local constables and their cohorts should be treating them as if they had done something wrong.

Well, as you can imagine, they did not find Irish O'Riley, O'Toole or any other WWI pilot on the premises. Tank was beginning to get agitated and feeling a bit embarrassed when nothing was turned up and no answers could be found. You see, although Irish O'Toole never admitted to Maryann, her family or any of the townspeople, the word as sent by Tank and Neidermeyer, was that Irish was a robber of the very banks that they had grown to hate during this depression. They didn't need an organized resistance, yet when the locals saw a need by one of their "own" for some help, they all were more than happy to oblige and help a likable guy, who was also a Hero of the Great War!

Maryann had a child that summer, and named him Robert Emil Gross. He was tall with broad shoulders and red hair. Everyone called him Reg.

No one ever asks.......... and the farm is still called The Emil Gross Family Farm.

CHAPTER 14

The Cement Mixer in High Society

We must have driven 600 miles over the last two and half weeks. No interstate, just state roads looking for an interesting lead. Illinois is not my nor Pat's birthplace. Nope, both of us were born in St. Louis Missouri. We wound up in Illinois after I made a side trip one day. You see, I was in an investment club at the time when we lived in Florissant Missouri. A beautiful place. Both of our children were born at St. John's Mercy Hospital. So, our investment strategy was changed the day some guy in Chicago won $44 million dollars with a $1 dollar chance on the Illinois Lotto ticket. My new duty in the investment club, since I lived the closest to Illinois, was to drive there every week and buy $400 worth of Lotto tickets. Quick end to that lead. We didn't win any money, BUT, I found a beautiful home designed by the famous Architect William Flippo, on the high bluffs of the Mississippi River. All glass on two stories, it was our retirement home bought first! We love it! And it is from here, that all of these stories have started. It's always easy to leave here, because we have so much to look forward to in returning to this place. So.....

Some days we strike gold. Most days it's just a wash and sometimes we go for weeks without a solid lead. As I said, we've just come off one of those periods.

At the start of this week, we found one. I was driving and before I knew it, Pat turned and said: "Stop. Go back."

I wondered what I had missed. I found a wide spot in the road, turned the car around and retraced my steps. It is a wonder that this big vehicle can turn in such a short radius. Just a little bit more than two lanes. It really surprises a lot of people when they see me try it, but how ya gonna know if ya ain't never? Always loved that old saying I heard from a good friend years ago.

Anyway, I still didn't see what piqued her interest as she guided me, "Slow down. There! See it?". I'll be darned if I saw anything so I pulled the car over and searched through the windshield…...still nothing. This area was a bend in the road and it was heavily wooded on both sides. I followed her to the other side of the road. She pointed and nodded up in the distance. Yes, I could see something. Sort of like a very ornate horse barn I could make out through the trees on a hill at least a mile in the distance. It was hidden for sure. It took a little walking and cocking and craning my neck, but there was definitely something there. Something worth investigating.

We could not determine any entrance or where we might find egress to this property. We drove down a lot of roads here and each one, though it looked promising at first, eventually turned the wrong direction and we were always forced back to start over. This went on for about an hour or two until, unnoticed by us, the afternoon had turned to dusk. We headed to the next town to find lodging for the night and set out to find a meal.

A real diner! We found a real old fashion diner made out of a railroad car right in the middle of southern Illinois!. We just couldn't pass this one up. We went in well past the dinner rush, but were welcomed anyway. We chose to sit at the counter and watch the grill. The cook was wearing a white hat/hair net and there was a half-chewed cigar hanging from his mouth. He was hard at work with a scraper on the griddle. Marge, who worked the counter, told Eddie to lose the stogie…."we got paying customers!" Eddie must have muttered something that I certainly didn't hear, but it sure set Marge off! She lit into him like a hornet that just had its nest kicked. She finally wrestled the cigar, or what was left of it, from Eddie. I heard him say some unintelligible words, but I did hear "Chef" at least once.

When Marge turned to us she had a cigarette hanging from her lips and said "Know the difference between a cook and a chef?" It wasn't a question I was supposed to answer. She blurted out "a cook has tattoos!" Eddie muttered something else and disappeared into the back. We looked at the menu and remarked about The Beef Wellington. Marge said not to get our hopes up as Eddie just wraps an elongated hamburger patty into a hotdog bun and toasts it. Eddie yelled from the back, something about his secret sauce. We also decided to skip the sushi and tried to find a traditional American dish (that we would feel safe with). You know, something that is cooked hot enough to ward off any little microbes Eddie may have missed with his scraper. We also decided we should get something that had as little contact with Eddie's hands as possible. We saw some Campbell's canned soup on the shelf and felt safe with that and some toast. After she served the soup, Pat asked Marge about the ornate horse barn or building that you could just barely make out from the state road.

She raised her eyebrows when she turned and asked "Why?" "We saw it from the road a couple of hours ago and we looked for a way to get closer and we could not find one. So we were just curious", Pat explained. By this time Eddie had come out muttering something about staying away and that they were never any good for the town. "Who was never any good for the town?" I asked.

"Reynolds Sheradan and his bunch," Eddie said. "That family has been trying to run things in this county their way for as long as my family has been here."

The rest of the meal was interspersed with our questions about the property and the family. Marge was easy enough to talk to about it, but Eddie had a certain toughness about him that we were not about to agitate. We stayed on having dessert and coffee. Having noticed the ashtrays sitting on a lot of the tables, I asked if they would mind if we sat there and had a smoke before we headed back to the hotel. Since they were just starting to close up, Marge said "suit yourself."

We saw that there was a bar across the street and we decided to try it for a nightcap. As we were leaving I asked if they would like to join us. "I would sure like to hear some more about the Sheradan family." Didn't get much response from either of them.

The bar's name was "The Office" and at one time may have been a name that fooled someone.....back in the 80's, but now it was just very old, not nostalgic old, but "should have been redecorated at least twice but it wasn't" old. There was heavy metal playing on the internet juke box and a couple of underaged drinkers were playing pool. There was one drunk at a side table trying his best lines on the old broad who had seen too many dawns walking out of a place like this. She still wore her hair in a pony tail and flung it around like a high school girl, much to the amusement of the drunk guy hitting on her.

We sat at the bar and had a couple of beers while we decided what to do next. We thought we would probably just call the area up on Google Maps and see if we could find the entrance that way. I had brought in an old road map that I was looking at. Pat was peeling the label off her bottle of Stag. The bartender pretended not to, but he was listening to our conversation. Just then Eddie walked through the door and looked around. He came over and said, "I thought I'd join you. A little bit of Marge goes a long way."

We bought him a beer and he exchanged pleasantries with Bill the bartender. Eddie asked us again why we were interested in the Sheradan place. This time Bill decided to join us. We explained our book project and told them about some of the interesting things and people we had already met. Things were kind of quiet while we were talking, and Eddie nodded towards the old drunk with the 50 year old cheerleader on the other side of the room; "That's him".
"Who?" I asked.
"Reynolds Sheradan." Said Eddie.
"The guy who owns that spread?" Pat asked.
"One and the same" said Bill, "He went downhill fast when his daddy disappeared."

In describing Reynolds, I thought that I would just quote Eddie who said that "Reynolds was a fat fuck with greasy, slicked back, black dyed hair, whose pudgy fingers looked like a ten pack of Armour hot dogs." I couldn't have done a better job....

Eddie looked at Bill and said, "That was the biggest fucking funeral I ever saw!" Eddie nodded in agreement, "And don't forget about the cement mixer."

Wait a minute. What cement mixer? WHAT CEMENT MIXER?

The kids on the pool table were getting louder. So was the music. Watching the pool game, it became apparent that someone was losing and not at ALL happy about it. Bill saw the money on the table. He jumped that bar with a corkball bat and cracked it on the side of the table with as much noise as threat. "I told you assholes no gambling in here! Now get out!" A bottle shattered on the floor. By now Reynolds Sheradan was heading into the action.

"What's going on here Bill, these kids aren't doing any harm. Just leave them be. Here, I'll buy a round for the house", as he peeled off a fifty from a roll of bills from his pocket. It became quite apparent that Reynolds still had a little pull in this town as Bill stashed the fifty in his shirt.

Reynolds stumbled back to the now enamored cheerleader. The pool players racked the balls for another game and Bill pulled out 3 Stags for us, and poured 4 shots.

After we all said "cheers" and took a shot, Eddie grabbed my arm. He could see that I was just about to ask Bill if he forgot about the round for the others and just gave me the look to "mind my own business."

Throughout the night we learned a little bit more about the Sheradans and some of the other town folks. At 10:30 a group of workers from the cat food plant down the street came in for a few shots. Around 11:30 the pool players got out of hand again and Bill threw them out half a game into 8-ball. The county sheriff came in around 12PM and, seeing no problems, quickly left. The pool players came back around 1:15 with a few more reinforcements, but they could barely walk, so Bill thought nothing about rousting them again.

Right before we decided to settle up and pay the tab, a whopping thirteen dollars, Bill motioned to Sheradan to come over and have a shot with us. He introduced us to Sheradan, who saw no reason to even look at us while Bill was pouring the shot. He downed it and walked towards the door.

Bill said "Prick".

Sheradan belched on his way out.

Eddie then decided that this was the time to tell us all about the Reynolds Sheradan family.

It seems that this little town on the eastern Illinois border was about halfway between Chicago and Indianapolis. During Prohibition, the Chicago Mob was instrumental in setting up distribution points of their bootleg whisky and other liquor they either made, bought from Canada or flat-out stole. Indianapolis was a thirsty town back then and the Chicago boss, Johnny Torrio, who later turned the entire business over to Al Capone, wanted a midway point for his delivery trucks to refuel, rest and/or hide out. Misty Sheradan, one of the girls hanging around Chicago back then, told them about her hometown and that it was a perfect place to hide out his distribution syndicate. Misty's father was a small town mayor who had no control over his daughter and her wild crowd. She convinced him to turn a blind eye to some of the trucks and seedier characters who were soon rolling into town. Misty's brother Ritchie had a mind for business and saw an opportunity here. He went to Chicago and with Misty's help pitched their hometown as a great home away from home as a Gangsters Retreat. He bought some property on the east end of town, 600 acres to be specific, to hedge his bet. Rumors were abounding in the 20's and Al Capone himself was known to frequent this resort, fronting money to Ritchie to set it up just the way he wanted it.

Ritchie knew how to deal with the mob. Ask what they want, then give it to them. Capone was only too happy to front the money for this project. He was a modern day Bugsy Segal, only in a small little Illinois town far from what was to become Las Vegas.

Ritchie liked horses and Capone liked to gamble on horses, or he liked it when others gambled because "the house" always wins. Ritchie was soon raising horses and built an elaborate race track, casino and restaurant where the Chicago boys would always be welcome. A hotel on the property insured them that they would be self-sufficient and as long as they kept the locals out and the sheriff in, they should be comfortable. Ritchie and the Chicago boys and the Indianapolis clients all became cozy with the arrangement. When Al went to prison in 1933, his gang continued to run the downstate operations.

However, Ritchie, with his new family, felt the strain of keeping up appearances even though most of the support from Chicago was not forthcoming any longer. Ritchie's only son Reynolds was born in 1949. They had lost the race track and closed the hotel by then due to declining popularity. The casino was never legal and had been gradually phased out by Ritchie who still wanted to stay on the right side of the law. Old habits die hard and there were brushes with the law although Ritchie always had a way out. The property was looking tired and run down. Misty and Ritchie, a shrewd businessman in his own right, put money away for the future generations, however many or few there would be. Both Ritchie and his sister envisioned a large family operation that would continue to bring income and wealth to the family, but that was not to be. There were no more children for whatever reason. These guys telling us the story had no idea why.

Ritchie realized the numbers racket and bootlegging were nowhere near as profitable as it once was. So the family business turned to loaning money out to the locals at exorbitant rates. This worked off and on for years, but they were always one step forward two steps back.

Reynolds Sheradan was a mediocre student through school and although the family gave off an "air" of wealth, they were nothing special any longer to the populace of the community. Reynolds would find himself face down in the playground gravel more than once each school year. When college came around, he chose a university in Miami Florida, because, well, you know, he liked to party. Oh, did he party.

While he was known to deal a little pot in high school, when he hit Miami Beach, he went big time. Kilos of pot were soon too small and he found a supplier in Mexico who could meet his needs. It wasn't long before, on a week-long "coke" binge, he decided he should fly to Medellin Colombia and pitch his story to an up and coming drug dealer you may have heard of down there in the 70's.

El Padrino wanted nothing to do with him and sent him away embarrassed.

He had dropped out of school in the middle of his junior year and there were a few investigations into his dealings and before they could turn to his father, he had confessed and taken a plea deal for 25 years for his distribution ring of pot and cocaine dealers throughout southern Illinois.

If grade school was bad for Reynolds Sheradan, the maximum security federal prison in New York was a street fighting school for anyone who needed to blow off a "little steam". Reynolds seemed to be getting his ass handed to him at least once a month, and with the added trouble, came added time.

When he was finally released in 2007, his total time served had gone from 25 years to 33 years. He had been treated for many broken bones, lacerations and infections during his incarceration. No one was on his visitor list. He had an attorney provided to him by the family trust still run by Ritchie. Ritchie had never really had any faith in Reynolds and left the trust to the control of his favored Chicago law firm. They let loose a little money in the form of an allowance each month and Reynolds would piss it away and be waiting impatiently a couple of days before the end of each month for the next check to arrive. He had numerous arguments with his father when, by chance,

Ritchie answered the phone AND accepted the call from the federal prison in Otisville.

Ritchie was not happy at all with the cards life had dealt him and was even more pissed that his moron of a son was doing more time than sentenced because his "candy ass" couldn't take care of himself.

Reynolds had filled out his release forms indicating that he would be living at home with Ritchie when the time came. Only when the administrator called Ritchie to confirm this fact, Ritchie was far from surprised and cursed and swore into the phone until he was drooling out the side of his mouth. His blood pressure must have been VERY high after that call.

Reynolds was put on hold in the system until they could figure out what to do, but, Ritchie had a change of heart (if he really had one) and finally called the Bureau of Corrections back and said that he was indeed going to have Reynolds live there with him.

Not too much was seen of either Ritchie or Reynolds Sheradan when he returned from prison in 2007.

It was sometime around 2011 that there was a series of peculiar events. Reynolds had a swimming pool torn out and replaced with a much larger Olympic sized lap pool. No big deal, but Reynolds supervised the whole thing. The locals remember Reynolds would argue and sometimes even get into fights with the tradesmen doing the work.

No one had seen Ritchie for a while by now and to squash rumors, Reynolds filed a missing persons report on his father. In 2018,

Reynolds legally had him declared dead and even had a memorial funeral at the local mortuary. Everyone in town came. A few older people came in from Chicago that no one really knew, but there were also a few younger people from Chicago, or so they announced. Now these boys wouldn't say HOW they knew Ritchie, but that they needed to pay their respects.

There were a couple of unsubstantiated rumors that did not interest the police.

One was the secrecy of the pool being replaced.

There was a rumor that another hole for a second pool may have been dug INSIDE of the horse barn, but there were absolutely NO workers that had ever seen or heard of this second pool.

And thirdly, Reynolds got into a big fight with the concrete contractor, although it was dismissed as self defense, the contractor was left in a coma for years before he died. After everything was settled with the contractor's estate, they were missing one cement mixer. They could account for all of the other large equipment, but nothing about the Frieghtliner 2014 114SD concrete mixer nor its driver ever turned up.

By now we were all pretty tired and decided to call it a night. We went back to our room and fell asleep talking about whether or not we should try and meet Reynolds in person at his compound.

We got up the next morning and went back to the diner car. Eddie was not there but Marge was. And not too happy to see us either. "I hope you feel as bad as Eddie looks," she said. Thoughts of him getting mugged by Reynolds flashed through both of our minds before she said, "He just ain't used to drinking like you city folks." Then she winked at us. She said he passed out on the couch whenever he came in this morning and is still there as far as she knew. She also said that she was the chef in the family, because Eddie had the tattoos. We ordered the "Farmers Breakfast platter", eggs, toast, bacon, and sausage, with a side of biscuits and gravy. When you are hung over and there are no Jack in the Box tacos, a big greasy breakfast is the next best thing.

We told Marge that we met Reynolds Sheradan last night and were thinking about trying to meet up with him to verify some of the stories and clarify some of the muddiness brought on by an 18 pack of Stag and 12 or so shots.

"That would explain Eddie's predicament", she said.

"Well," Marge yawned, "you might want to rethink that trek to the Sheradan's. Reynolds is not only nasty, but down right dangerous. Although no one around here will admit to knowing anything about it, everyone in town knows that Reynolds Sheradan killed his father and put him in a cement mixer buried under the floor of that horse barn that you were so interested in yesterday. I mean, what other conclusion can you jump to? The missing cement truck, the extra hole, and don't forget the old man went missing at about the same time," she slowly pointed out one finger at a time while listing these points. "Yeah, I'd leave it to the FBI or CIA or whoever handles bad-asses nowadays."

Of course, most people have short memories and really are more concerned with themselves than others, so it seemed that once again, discretion was to be the better part of valor, so we enjoyed our greasy breakfast, left Reynolds Sheradan alone and headed out for another story.

It was quite quiet on the ride back home as we both contemplated this last one......

CHAPTER 15

Victor the Wrestling Bear

*P*at and I had seen road signs directing us towards a small town advertising the off-season storage facility of "American Royalty Shows". We were familiar with this carnival from when we were kids. It would pass through the St. Louis area, hoisting its tents on some vacant truck lots on Hall Street. It was just a large collection of sideshows and freak shows that would have been peeled off the midway of a major circus when they were no longer up to the quality that circuses require of their sideshows. But what really sent us up here was my new friend Max. He called me out of the blue and said that he had a lead if I wanted to follow up on it. It seems that at one time his agency had represented "Victor the Raslin' Bear." Victor has since passed, but his trailer and the trainer's trailer were last seen at "American Royalty Shows" seasonal storage yard in southern Illinois.

After a three hour drive, we pulled into the storage yard which turned out to be just a siding off an abandoned spur in another desolate town in southern Illinois. Hardly the winter home of other well known circuses and traveling carnivals found in the warmer southern climates.

We found the yard manager Carl in the bar where Max said he would be, and after a bit of discussion that was going nowhere, I suggested that we treat him to lunch so we could talk a bit more about it. That sounded good to Carl and he led us next door to a little greasy spoon with a sputtering neon sign that just said "EATS".

Carl went for the menu and when the waitress came over, he looked at us and said, "You're buying , right?". I nodded and he put the menu down and ordered a Johnny Walker, neat, and went to polishing his spoon with his shirt.

The waitress came back with his scotch. Pat and I felt safe ordering the cheeseburger, and as we finished ordering, Carl put his glass down and just said, "another."

It was well after noon so I didn't expect to see many people in this desolate stretch of hell, but we were surprised to see a few people come in on this cold winter day. As they walked past, each person acknowledged Carl with a bit of reverence. Apparently Carl was the go-to guy to get anything done with American Royalty Shows back in the day. Although it still makes its yearly tour in the summer, now it mostly travels around the midwest, rarely traveling out of a four state area. The train cars are just storage now as trucks, pickups and campers are the main form of transportation for this specific freak show. Carl was keeping track of the carnies here that he would need to collect in the spring to take off on the next tour.

By the time we had our cheeseburgers, Carl had downed another four Johnny Walkers, all on my tab. Good thing that they did not have Blue Label. Carl turned to me and asked, "How is that old SOB Max nowadays, did he ever amount to anything? Last time I saw him he was trying to get Victor the Raslin' Bear out on a summer road trip with some fly-by-night rock and roll show. That man could surely pick 'em." I figured that Carl would be much happier thinking that Max was indeed a much greater failure than he was, so I just let it pass. Now, here is where you should have gone back to the Preface where you should realize that what I said in the second paragraph was true. As I have read back on this many times, I always stop and think that this last sentence may leave you thinking that Max did not amount much. Well, Max was indeed a great man. Charles "Max' Million, go ahead. Look him up. I'll wait.

Back now? Ok then.

It has been about four years since I had written this and now, after Max has passed, I feel much sorrow for my loss and the loss of the ENTIRE music community. I only wish that I had met him earlier in my life. Who knows, we could have taken over the world. You DO know that being of German Heritage, if you do not think of taking over the world at least once a month, they take away your "Card"!

Well, that's how we found out about Victor. Carl took us over to a couple of the trucks and trailers stashed here and there around this small town and showed us Victor's trailer. Not much to look at now, however, you could see that Victor, even though a bear, did carry some weight in this show. Carl told us that he was way above the other side shows and freaks. Victor and his trainer actually made money on these runs.

The trailer that Victor had was laid out pretty well. The PETA people followed this act on occasion and would make their presence known with an occasional protest with people carrying signs and banners. According to Carl this was not as much a bother as free publicity which they took in stride with each occurrence. Victor's trainer back then had a relatively nice set up as well with his own trailer towed behind his large pickup with duallies and a "Cat" diesel. The trainer's trailer even had a very nice sound system in it for the time. Carl said that the trainer and Victor would relax after the show by listening to Vivaldi and sipping Courvoisier, the trainer, not Victor. No, Victor would relax with his favorite, a bowl of Pabst Blue Ribbon and a couple of salmon that they always had in their freezer. All in all, a good life for both.

Victor never had any real stress in his life and the trainer liked to keep it that way. Carl said that many a time he would knock on the door in the morning to roust everyone to get moving to the the next site, and Victor and the trainer would be passed out and slowly move back to normal after a morning walk which usually scared the shit out of any locals who may have wandered by in the AM. But, back to the show.

You see, Victor would sit in his cage looking harmless and docile all the while the barker was extolling the strength in just his paws, razor sharp wit and killer-like tendencies. Later towards the evening he would start offering a $20 bill to the first person who was brave enough to get into the wrestling ring with Victor. Everyone after this would have to pay $5 for this chance because if the rube was lucky enough to actually pin Victor, they would get a brand new $100 bill. Carl even waved a bill around his head here in "EATS" just to show us how it was done.

Well, there were a couple of points you should know here, that Max already clued us into. First of all, you could not ever pin a Bear because of the anatomy of the animal. Their shoulders just do not come together so as to be pressed on the mat at the same time. Another point Max had told us, was that they used to feed Victor onions which made for some very awful breath if you were dumb enough to get near him. He did wear a muzzle so as not to actually have anymore of an advantage than the rube would figure out.

Oh, and the onions did not do too much for his digestive tract either, so that most of the time, Victor had already taken a big greasy dump on the mat just as the money transaction had taken place. Now who in their right mind would want to get down on the mat with that mess and smelly bear? Lastly, Victor was not too keen on being there in the first place and just wanted to be left alone. It only took him a couple of minutes to get tired of this game and give his opponent one good swipe with his taped paws to send him flying face first into a pile of bear excrement. All good for a laugh and the paying customers would always bring in a couple of hundred dollars a night for this unrehearsed ballet. Victor never lost a match.

Well that was it. Not much of a story. I hope that you were as pleasantly surprised as Pat and I were.

But be glad that it didn't cost you $45.00 for Carl's Johnny Walker tab that day.

CHAPTER 16

Start The Caddy
I Need A Drink

*R*emember back in the first story? I was drinking with Joe Hubbard? The banjo player? Well, Joe had tracked me down a few months back and gave me a lead on an interesting story. It seems one of his old friends that he used to play with, was retired and living across the Wabash in Indiana, and although it was not going to be an Illinois Barn Story, Joe thought that I would get a kick out of stopping by and visiting Denny Ray. According to Joe, Denny is one of the most down to earth people you will ever want to come across, and with a snicker in his voice, ended with, "and you need to ask to see his old car out under the shed." Joe said that he had already talked to Denny and he would be expecting a call from me. Presumptuous on Joe's part, but I took Denny's number down and called him about a week later.

Denny answered the phone with a short, Tennessee,"Hey," I replied with "What up cupcake?" just to set him off edge a bit. I could tell he had a smile on his face when he said, "I've been expecting your call. Y'all coming on over?"

After a half hour of horsing around on the phone like Joe told me we would be doing, I got his address and decided on driving over on a Sunday morning to catch him at his god-awful worst. Joe was right, he liked to drink a bit.

When I showed up at his home no more than 100 feet from the Wabash River, again I could tell I had met a fellow drunkard and musician. Denny opened the door to his river cabin holding a Mason jar of white lightning in his hand. "Just to take the edge off," he said. After assuring him I was neither the feds nor the Baptists, he let me in after insisting I "take a swig" so we are both on an even keel. He picked up his guitar and handed me another one.

I looked at it with a puzzled look on my face I guess and Denny, said; "Joe told me you were a musician."
I explained that I was, but I did not play guitar.
Now it was Denny's turn to look puzzled at me. Imagine, a musician who DOESN"T Play GUITAR? Pronounced "Git-ar" down these parts…

We got past that awkward part after a few moments and Denny settled down on an old living room couch, maybe his great grandmother's for all I knew, the way it smelled…….I guess it didn't help that it seemed to have a permanent resident living on it; Denny's dog Sophie. She was an old hillbilly hound dog as close as I could tell. Her tail would wag when Denny would talk, although she wasn't that much interested as she never once bothered to lift her head up to even acknowledge me.

I mentioned that Sophie must be a hell of a watchdog. Denny continued *that* thought to tell me that if he as much as heard *any* loud noise in the middle of the night, all he had to do was to wake up Sophie and she would bark like hell..........Anyway, Denny opened up and played a few of his songs and then switched to banjo for some up-beat pickin'.

By this time the 'shine' had warmed me up considerably and I explained the project that I was working on. Denny seemed easy enough listening to my stories and interjecting some well placed banjo or guitar tacets.(a real word, although my computer keeps flagging it thinking that I am doing a plumbers job and offers me "Faucet". Which actually seems like a fit considering what I am soon about to tell you.) Denny got up and said we had to go check on the *trot* lines and *jigs* he had set last night before he left to play at the local bar.

After a short walk up river a bit to an old creek we waded through some mud and muck to find nothing on any of them. It would not have surprised me if Denny just forgot the bait last night. I wasn't about to point this out and let him mumble to himself about 'the goddamn smart son of a bitch' fish' they had around there. It seems though, they weren't all that smart when Denny was younger.

Walking back to the cabin, empty handed, except for the now almost empty Mason jar, I casually mentioned that Joe said something about an old Caddy he had stashed away under a shed. As soon as the words came from my mouth I realized that I may have spoken out of turn. He had stopped and started to defend himself. No, this car was not stashed, it had no sinister or even questionable past. I found myself shuffling around trying to smooth the waters and when Denny started chuckling, it was then that I figured that once again, he was just playing me.

Denny side tracked me over to a lean-to shed where he had a 1976 White Cadillac El Dorado. This thing must have been something in its prime, but now there wasn't an un-dented body panel on this car. Both tail light lenses were not gone as much as smashed so that there was less red and more white showing. I suspect that Denny had taped some red cellophane over one and a piece of a broken red solo cup over the other. The vinyl top was ripped in so many places that it looked like a skirt Pat Benatar wore on her "Love is a Battlefield" video. And the smell? I asked what it was and Denny gave me a wink as he told me the story.

Denny was not only a tremendous picker, he appeared on the Grand ole' Opry on a weekly basis in the 60's through the 80's, but he also was a top moonshiner in eastern Kentucky in his early days. He had done some time, having been caught making it, selling it, transporting it and of course drinking it. According to Denny, he must have spent the better part of his adult life in jail in one county or another. He compared it to a life sentence on the installment plan. Denny just had this penchant for alcohol to fuel his frenzied picking and needed the 'shine in his bloodstream, or as I have seen, needed to keep a little blood in his alcohol stream.

When he opened up the hood, I recognized some extra plumbing and piping running around the engine compartment that then disappeared into the firewall. He showed me the glove box which was devoid of the expected tickets, registrations and license renewal notices that you would see in most glove boxes. No, this one had a manifold of valves and switches and a pressure gauge with a piece of masking tape colored red with a magic marker with the words DANGER marking a specific area.

Then he opened up the trunk. There was a very compact, and very corroded copper kettle still in the large expanse of what served as a trunk back then. I thought I recognized it though. A real, honest to god, moonshine still, although on a much more compact basis. Denny had managed to include a working still, that was heated by the engine coolant through a custom made heat exchanger. There were copper tubes running everywhere! There was a vat for the mash, which he made and fermented at home and once a week, he would load the whole mess into this El-Dorado Caddy and drive to the Opry. According to him, by the time he reached Nashville, the mash was all cooked off, which he just dumped by the side of the road, and proceeded to enjoy a fresh batch of moonshine every night right before he was to go on. Of course all the people on the Opry knew what he was up to, and some even looked forward to partaking of his delicacy each trip. He usually kept one jar hidden so that he would even have one on the drive back.

The car is not up to safety standards these days, but Denny's picking sure is. I will be looking forward to seeing him when he gets his call for the old timers show at the Opry coming up this decade.
If he hasn't killed himself.
I watched him drive.

He's a maniac.

CHAPTER 17

But Where Is
He Buried?

*G*reat breakfast to start the day; a warm Pepsi and some cookies. Gotta start finding better hotels, at least one with a breakfast buffet, but then again, those are kinda hard to find under $40 a night..........

Well, it's 9 AM and I am confronted with the first choice of the morning, head north on the interstate to head somewhere else, or stay on the state roads and keep digging around here. Nothing to do anyway, so those choices really don't make much difference. I mean when you wake up with nothing to do and it's only half finished when you go to bed, you have a certain flexibility in your life.

About two hours down the road I see one of these old, side of the road Standard Service Stations that used to populate the state highways back in the 20's through the 1960's. You know the ones; all brick (at least here in Tornado Alley) with a roof overhang out to the pair of gas pumps. This one was white and red shiny subway brick panels. On the right side there were two large glass panel roll up doors, one for each bay. On the left side was a door that was propped open with a dirty stick and then a floor to ceiling glass window continued on to the side of the building. There was a large crack running from the base of the window, up toward the side of the door. It ended about 5 foot up and had been covered with a piece of duct tape for, you know; safety and aesthetics.

Although it showed its age, you could see that it was once a proud Standard Oil of Ohio Service Station, but not yet caught up to the age of electronics with digital red lights screaming the price per gallon at you. No, this one has a sandwich board sign that needs the price changed as often as the price of gas changes. Someone was just bending over and inserting the last of the "cents" price when I pulled up.

"Hardly seems worthwhile putting in that 9/10 cents these days"? I asked, opening my car door.

Keith looked at me like I had two heads. His shirt announced who he was, but I guess he could have just been wearing what was left in the "clean" bin. For all I know his name could have been Gary or Denny, but he looked like a Keith.

It had been raining all morning and I didn't necessarily want the interaction, so I just twisted the metal knob to reset the "regular" pump, then cranked the handle to turn on the pump, grabbed the nozzle, stuck it in and squeezed the operating lever and finally clicked the hold open latch to let it fill up. Keith was one of the lone gas pump attendants left in southern Illinois I would imagine, and he gave me a certain look of disdain when he saw that I retained my gas pump knowledge from when I had that job back in the late 60's.

I stood under the leaky overhang and watched the cars traveling up and down the road, each leaving a mist of water, oil and road grime hanging in the air. The smells around a gas station are different these days, very little gasoline smell with all the filters and pollution mitigation equipment. My mind took me back to the early 1970's. When I worked at George's Standard Station, you could identify gasoline and motor oil, both new and burnt. Ninety weight gear lube, now that was the worst in my estimation. Transmission fluid, Dextron and Type F all had their own look, feel and odors. George swore that Dextron would grow a crop of pimples as it ran down his forearm when he was doing transmission work. Parts cleaner was always generously applied to everything to make you think that some great sterile operation was about to be performed, only to let it all fall to the floor and then get walked through and tracked all over. Even the grease for the lube jobs had a smell.

Oh yeah, don't forget to add in the shop dog who lived in whatever car whose door was left open. Ours was named Walter, the dog, not the car.. Now imagine, dumping these all on the floor every day, so that when it came that time of the month to clean it you had to use a long handled steel floor scraper. Wow! What a smell that was. Sometimes we weren't allowed in the front office because George said his wife wanted to keep it clean.

Walter had full run of our office and shop and even the small parts room which was really just a roped off area of the hard ceiling over the office. The rope was there to keep you from wandering out over the suspended ceiling which was covering the rest of the shop. Walter was thought of as part security, part mascot. He would greet everyone with the full expectation of a head pat or part of whatever you bought from the vending machine. His favorite was Fritos.

One Saturday night we had a really nice 1968 Chevy Impala 2 door convertible in the first bay next to the office. Fathom Blue Poly with a white convertible top. I had just driven it into bay 1 as we were getting ready to close and lock up for the weekend. George made sure to tell me to put up the top and roll up the windows so that Walter wouldn't sleep in it. I did and even went the extra mile to lock the doors just in case Walter could pick locks. A very long shot, but I was just making sure.

It was my turn to open up on Monday morning and I was there right on time, 6:45 for a 7 AM opening. George taught me, and everyone else who worked there, that preparing for work was on "my nickel, NOT his". It was always noted in any review from that point on that I was at least punctual and generous with my time. George was one who "shaped" my character in my younger years.

I opened the front door and went directly to the back office and changed into my clean uniform for the week, blue pants and a light blue shirt with my name on the right pocket. None of it really fit. Sort of a one size fits all. My dirty old shop shoes were just where I had kicked them off on Saturday night. I picked up the cash drawer and counted out the money to make sure it was correct. $30 in singles, $50 in fives, $50 in tens and 5 twenty's. A brand new roll of 50 pennies, 50 nickels, and 25 quarters. Seems right. I heard George walk in the front office and start calling Walter.

Holy shit! I didn't check on Walter! When I came up the half stairs from the back office, I saw George standing next to the Impala, looking in the passenger window and shaking his head. I wondered who was sitting in the driver's seat until it became obvious.

HOW THE HELL DID THAT STUPID DOG GET INTO THE CAR I HAD LOCKED? When I got to the front of the car, Walter had his ears down and was now standing on the once immaculate white upholstered seats with his greasy black paws and wagging his tail. Before I could exclaim my innocence, George turned to me half laughing and pointed to the ceiling!?! The dog had gone up stairs over the office and jumped onto the suspended ceiling which in no way would hold the weight of a full grown Shepherd mix. He fell straight through the ceiling and through the white convertible top. George said I guess we need to close off the stairs every night......Walter wasn't particularly clean and with the torn top and pretty much ruined upholstery, well, George owned another car that day.

Returning to the present when the pump handle in my hand clicked off telling me that my gas pump duties for today's trip were coming to an end, I noticed a woman in an older Cadillac, windshield wipers going full blast, flinging rain water on either side of the car. She pulled under the canopy between the pumps and the office. As she rolled down her window, she looked at Keith and said: "Check my right tire?" It was more of a command than a request. Keith didn't even move from leaning against the open door frame when he said, "IT'S RAINING LADY! GO TO SHELL!"

I walked into the front office to pay as Keith disappeared into the shop. The owner I guess was just finishing up a job and wiping his hands on a red shop towel and walking in to greet me. I nodded my head towards Keith and raised my eyebrows while looking at the owner. He just shrugged his shoulders as he handed me back $4.50 from the $50 that I gave him for the gas.

"It's the wife's kid," he said. "What can I do?"

I dropped the 2 quarters he gave me into the vending machine and had to slap it once on the side to get my Payday. He had been watching me get my gas and understood that we had a connection to old gas stations; he, however, never moved on.

I wasn't particularly itching to get back on the rainy road either, so I asked him about a rusted-out hulk of an old 1969 road runner that I saw alongside the building when I used the "restroom". Oh yeah, I'm sure you have been in worse, so let's just say this one hasn't won any Good Housekeeping seal of approval. At any rate, he didn't seem to want to talk about the friendly molecules of rust holding hands just to keep the shape of an old MOPAR long enough so that one more person might recognize it.

I know how to get to this guy; I asked him to change a couple of bucks so I could get a soda out of his vintage Pepsi machine. This one had the door on the side with the bottles laying horizontal. I told him how we had to move ours back inside in the summer when the kids found out they could come up at night with a dixie cup and a bottle opener and have half a free bottle anytime we weren't looking. His eyebrows raised as he gave me a sideways glance. I went for the old combination 1-2 and asked him if he wanted a cold one, and then said that we used to keep beer in the back of ours.

He was smiling as he walked over, fished out a chain from his pocket with at least a million keys on its ring and proceeded to open the screw lock on the side of the box. As the door gently swung open, I could see a six pack of Stag Beer bottles in the bottom. He took one and gave one to me and we both sat down on the blue, front bench seats from what may have been a blue 1969 vintage Mopar. Who knows, it could have been from a Road Runner.

We toasted what was left of the morning looking out at the rain. "Name's Rick", my new friend said.

Keith came in and said he was going down to get some lunch at the Arby's down on the interstate. I was remembering how much I enjoyed the lunches at the service station back in the 60's. I said, you know, the station used to be quite a meeting place when I was working as a mechanic in the 60's. We used to pool some money and I would walk down to Bovay's Confectionary on Diamond Drive and buy a pound of salami, a pound of American cheese and a fresh loaf of bread. Those were some of the best sandwiches that I can remember. The grease stains wherever my fingers touched the bread didn't spoil the feast, at least as I remember it. Rick looked at me, pulled out a five and said let's walk across the street. The store was a lot bigger than the confectionery that I had remembered, but it had well worn wooden floors and smelled like smoked meats.

We pooled our two five dollar bills and bought my old recipe, smiling all the way back to the office, walking through the rain. And no, for the ten dollars of our lunch pool, we didn't get near a pound of anything, just enough to make a couple of sandwiches. One nice thing about a small town, you can walk away from your business to get lunch and no one will think twice about it.

Those sandwiches were just as tasty but a lot cleaner than I remember them when I made them for Rick and myself that day. Other than Rick dipping his in a bottle of hot mustard before each bite, I could have been back at the old Standard station if I'd closed my eyes.

I thought I would try one last story on Rick to see if I could get him to open up about the Road Runner. Besides, he had offered me another Stag. "Ever see a '32 Ford come through here?" I asked. Rick agreed that those were some cool cars, but a bit before his time. Well, of course they were before my time too, I said and plunged into another memory.

Fridays we always closed the station about 7 PM, cleaned up and then got into the beer. We would see anywhere between 5-12 people after hours on Friday evening. I am certain that some other transactions were taking place, but I was smart enough to keep my nose out of any of those. It just so happens that at this time we had an old shell of a 1932 Ford in the shop, it belonged to the shop and George was still deciding what to do with it. After a few beers, I had a lot of the guys convinced that we could chop, channel and section that car. Good thing there was a liquor store next door, as I remember we sent out more than once for someone to restock our Pepsi machine.

Long about 10PM I must have gotten out a piece of chalk or most probably just a piece of drywall that we had broken off the wall for just this purpose. I got to work marking that car up with chalk lines for chopping the top. With all the free help that was there, I was encouraged to really get creative, which I did. We all called it a night sometime around 1AM and I walked back home. I had to open up the next morning, but I overslept and came walking in about 10 Saturday morning.

I walked into the office to get my clean uniform and could hear and see flashes of light as a cutting torch was dismembering this vintage machine. When I walked back to see it, George had precisely cut every line that I had marked.......in chalk......in a drunken stupor. All of the pieces to the roof were laid out on the floor and he twisted off the acetylene valve, the torch making the final "pop" just as I walked in and asked "What are you doing?" " What do you think?" George replied, looking at me like I was stupid. "We're starting that chopped and channeled Gasser we talked about last night. With a horrified look on my face, a quivering voice and a VERY LARGE lump in my throat, I explained that I had no idea what I was doing the night before and that I certainly didn't expect him to take a torch to it the first thing in the morning!

Well, he looked at the floor, started shaking his head. I thought I was fired, but he looked up and chuckled with a crooked little grin, and shortly had a full on belly laugh going. It was contagious and I caught it soon enough. We were standing there laughing and hitting each other on the back and shoulder until we were in tears. Then while he walked out the door, he turned to me and said in a very stern voice, "I'm taking the rest of the day off so I don't fire your stupid ass....... You clean up this mess. Nodding to the now pieced out '32 Ford Coupe"

To this day I'm not sure that this wasn't his original plan for the car anyway. I suspect it had a nefarious past......

Well, Now Rick was having a good laugh over this as well and then he decided to tell me the story about the Road Runner:

"You see," he started, "there were a few of us who hung out around this place when we were kids, you know before I started working here and eventually bought it after I came back from the Army." Rick went to Vietnam as a grunt and finally left as a member of a LRRP as designated by General Westmoreland. Long Range Reconnaissance Patrol taught many a grunt some very sophisticated and practical as well as impractical skills to come back to the States to begin their new adult life.

Rick came back home in 1967 and picked up right where he left off pumping gas and turning a wrench as needed. Some of the guys he had been running with had bought some cars and were into street racing. Long about 1969 one of his buddies, who kept losing, and Rick stressed this point strongly, he lost EVERY street race he ran driving his factory stock 1964 four door Plymouth Belvedere with the 225 cu in slant six. Rick said that his buddy wasn't that mechanically inclined, but he did replace the floor mats once.

Well "Builder", he got that name from working at the car shops doing piece work after high school, never did get the hang of winning with that car. One day without any other talk about it, he just showed up with a brand new 1969 Plymouth Road Runner with the 383 cubic inch engine with a four barrel carb, *but,* "and he stressed this next point excruciatingly:" with an automatic transmission and BENCH SEATS!!!!!. Thinking this would blow the doors off of anything running in this area, Builder proudly showed off his new "baby" to anyone who would listen. He didn't even get glass-packs on it, just factory exhaust! Rick said that Builder went from dating "ugly" chicks, to hot chicks within a week.

Soon Builder was seen with a new date every week! How could this be? According to Rick, this was simply because, although Builder had a hot car, the girls just didn't like being with him every time he lost. Every time, even the few times he would go up against a Rambler, he would lose. Either asleep at the wheel when the flag came down or just smoked the tires when he broke them loose. It became a standing joke at the town's Standard station every Saturday night before they closed and headed to the two lane blacktop at the north end of town for race night. Who would Builder lose to tonight? Not for lack of trying.

According to Rick, Builder had added Cragar Mag Wheels to his car and a high flow air cleaner. Even went so far as to buy some "Instant Horsepower Additive" for his gas tank, but nothing would improve this car's performance. Turns out that after about a year of this, talk turned to ways of getting rid of this "Lead Sled". Obvious problem was a screw lose behind the wheel.

Then it happened. Early one morning after Builder had gone to bed and parked his car alongside the house where he lived with his parents, his car was stolen. The police were called, reports were filed, insurance companies were involved and Rick said that they even took photographs of where the car USED to be parked! The police would call it the crime scene, but Rick to this day gets a kick out of the fact that they probably took the first picture of a "stolen" car! Builder eventually got a check for the value of the car, minus depreciation and deductible. He was still able to buy a respectable car to drive to the blacktop, although he never raced again.

Rick said that for years afterwards there was speculation as to why someone would steal such a dog of a car. Builder moved on, got married, owned a couple of businesses around the area before he passed away around 2000 from lung cancer. He was a smoker.

"So", is that what's left of the road runner?" I asked as I nodded towards the hulk. Rick just said, "and our couch here that we're sitting on."

It turns out that the "gang" had grand ideas as to what to do with the car before the job was done. Strip it down and sell the body panels to the body shops, part out the interior and chassis pieces and sell the drivetrain to whoever could move it. But AFTER, well that was another story. It seems that everyone who was involved got cold feet whenever a plan that wasn't theirs was discussed. All in all, the car sat covered in a friend's garage for almost 5 years before they decided to even move it. It then spent its life being towed or trailered from one garage to another, carport, backyard, open field and finally its last resting place, right here, where the original idea came up.

Rick took it as a gesture towards the memory of his old friend Builder back in 2004 and had it hauled here as it's final resting place. I asked where Builder was buried and Rick couldn't remember, but he will always know where his car is......

CHAPTER 18

There Was Devastation Everywhere, Men Were Dropping like Flies. Yeah, I Remember the Cola Wars

*W*e got another lead from Craigslist. Even though I pulled that ad down years ago, it still must be in a cache somewhere. It was a short message: "If you want to see what my stupid ex- husband left in our barn, contact Delma at---------; and she left a phone number. It took me a couple of days, but I made the call. I mean, the message did have all the makings of a good story. An ex-wife, a stupid ex-husband and a thing".. We were hooked.

Although she would not tell me anything about the story and no hints were to be had no matter how hard I tried, we agreed to meet her on her front porch at 10 am the next day. It was a long trip, a little over 3 hours, but still in the same area code. That's just the state of Illinois. A geographic oddity if ever there was one....

Pat told me to slow down. I'm a pretty safe driver these days. In my younger days, I worked for a New York based healthcare company named Technicon. My territory consisted of basically all the accounts in the midwest that my senior peers did not want for one reason or another. One such reason was an MD (Medical Doctor) who would get mad at the SMAC (Sequential Multiple Analysis Computer, think $175,000.00 in 1970's money) when it broke down, he would kick or throw a full metal trash can at it! My challenge for most of my days was to see how fast I could get from one town to the next.

At one point I had accumulated enough speeding tickets to get a nice letter from the Secretary of the State of Illinois advising me that if they caught me driving, not just speeding, but just driving in Illinois, they would arrest me, lock me up and throw away the key. No, these days I take it pretty safely and stay under the speed limits....except for today.

As luck would have it, I was pulled over and as the officer was checking my license, registration and priors, (he found nothing), so since I was already sitting in the front seat of the squad car, I made some small talk, thinking it may help. Turns out, that the police LIKE it when their 'perps' start talking and telling things that could be construed as evidence. Well, I told him the story about the last time I was in a squad car:

My family and I were vacationing in our cabin cruiser and wound up traveling down the Mississippi River, then left at Cairo and up the Ohio river, then right and upriver on the Tennessee River through the largest Lock Up into Kentucky Lake and still heading south and up the Tennessee River and finally to Paris Landing Tennessee at the local marina. Having cruised the last 3 days to get there. We were drawn to this particular marina, because its major attraction was a 1930s lodge built out of locally quarried stone by the CCC plus, the lodge was famous for its Friday night Seafood Buffet. We were instructed by the Harbormaster to just come up to the marina office whenever we were ready to go. Our party included Pat and me, my daughter Julie and her friend Tonya, both 14 years old, and another couple who were completing the trek with us in their houseboat.

At the appointed time, 5 pm I think, we were waiting on the dock and the manager said "I already called; here comes your ride". It was a Paris Landing Tennessee Police car. You know the ones, *the freedom from choice mobile*, no door handles on the inside passenger compartment, with a large bullet proof, Plexiglass partition between the front and back seat. Well, the female officer was nice enough about it and let my daughter and me sit in the front seat while everyone else had to pile into the back seat. The officer even let Julie turn on the siren when we pulled into the front of the lodge.

Now, this being some fairly large event in Paris Landing social year, there was a line around the front of the lodge which ran out into the parking lot. She pulls us right up to the front of the line, and gets out of the car to open all the doors for us. As we were all getting out,

I heard one of the people standing in line remark; "Now they treat their prisoners right nice down here!"

That story seemed to get a smile from the officer here who had pulled me over and I was let go with a short lecture about driving safely while I was here. Pat and I waved as we got back on the two lane and headed off towards our appointment with Delma. Pat told me to slow down at least one more time.

As we pulled up, she was standing on the porch with her arms crossed, a scowl on her face, and an unfiltered Camel cigarette hanging from her lips, with the ash just about to drop. I started to do the introduction, but she just said "Come on, I'll show you." Delma must have been in her late 40's or maybe even into her 50's. She had a pair of large gold hoop earrings with more than a few gold plated bracelets and necklaces. She wore platform shoes with her hair up in the latest Dallas TV style, I guess from the 1990's sometime. Must have put her a full head taller than most anyone else in our crowd . She must have had some warning with her about turning off ceiling fans, or else, maybe her friends just knew.

We followed her behind her house where she stopped to tend to some goats. It seems that Delma raised goats on this farm. She said that she had an agreement with a couple of families to work the land over the years after her ex, that would be Doug, "run off", but as the smaller farms made way for the larger corporate monstrosities, she just adapted and took to raising goats.

"I don't need much and what I can't grow or raise, the small income from goat milk, goat cheese and goat rental seems to keep me in the good graces of the protestants around here."

When I mentioned Larry McMurty and "Lonesome Dove" you know: *We don't rent no pigs.* She just looked at me, so I challenged her about goat rental.

"It's the darndest thing around here" she began, "you see, about 40 years ago one of the Porter boys got married and someone, mind you no one knows who, tied an old Billy goat to the gift table at the reception hall. Like I said no one knows anything about it, like who it was from or even how it got in there. Can you imagine? 200 people coming and going at a wedding and NOBODY saw a thing!!!? It was funny though watching the Porter boys trying to get that goat into a car to take back home. It never occurred to them to put it in the pickup that they all shared. That goat tore out half the back seat before they got it home."

"They kept it at their place for years as a watch goat. That goat was MEAN! It would take off after anyone for no reason at all. Tried to butt the preacher one Sunday after he came around to visit the boys' mother when she couldn't make it to services. After a few years, I offered to buy the goat from them as they were getting ready for a July 4th bar-b-que and had been eyeing that goat for a few weeks up to that. My ex, Doug got me a Nanny to go with that Billy and pretty soon we were up to our necks in goats. About 30 years later, pretty much everyone had forgotten about that wedding. A young man came up to me and asked if I could rent him a goat. I had never seen him before. "What on earth do you want to rent a goat for?" I asked. He said it was a secret and when I asked if it had to do with a wedding, he started giggling and turns out, someone had told him that story when he was a little boy and he had never forgotten about it. Now he has a good friend getting married a county over and thought it would be a great time! I couldn't find any reason not to rent the goat, so we agreed on a price and since I already knew the reception hall, The Antioch Baptist Church basement, I agreed to help him with the plan."

"You see, in the 1880's a con-man/architect came through and sold almost every Baptist church his unique, one of a kind, architectural plans for a brand new church. Of course with the blessing of the bishop, who I think was called "Coach"...... Only they ALL WERE THE SAME!!!!!

I knew that there was a back hallway that was always blocked off after they started building these churches. Most had been using it for storage. I knew that I could get the goat in there and hidden before any guests started showing up. I also knew that the gift table would be set back by the hallway. Always is. It's sort of off to the side, so when the time came, I just walked over, brought out the goat, who was not too keen on seeing that crowd, and tied him to the gift table and then walked out, no one the wiser. "

Since Doug had run off, and I could sure use the money, renting out goats seemed like a good idea. Now people w*ant them IN THEIR WEDDING*! Seems that's the magic potion, to get one as a gift. Imagine, I rent a goat out almost once a week to be in a wedding! They pick it up and they bring it back! FED! Money from Heaven!"

I smiled, shaking my head and asked if the architect was one of her relatives? She took a long drag on a recently lit Camel; Her tone turned almost hostile at that point. We were now walking towards her barn. I thought she had a sense of humor.

When I called, she said that she'd just as soon that all names, dates and places were left out and she turned to remind me of that.

She was mumbling something as we walked up to the barn, and with a few yanks, deft pulls and one well-placed kick, she finally got the door open. We walked in and saw all the stuff that one could accumulate in what, maybe a 40 something year life and maybe, 10-20 years marriage; I'm guessing now. Still with the scowl on her face and her arms crossed, she had ground out the Camel with her shoe a few steps before, she pointed to a truck. A big forty-something footlong Pepsi truck. You know, the ones from back in the 60's and 70's that had the slanted slide up doors in the side that held, maybe 800-1000 cases of Pepsi?

I said, "That truck?"

She screeched; "SEE! That's what my stupid ex-husband had left in our barn for all these years!"

Pat and I just looked at each other and then back to her. "Can you maybe explain a little bit so we can understand?"

Turns out the man Delma married was not the brightest bulb in the chandelier. They both worked, she as a cashier at the Zayre store down near the mall, and her "stupid" husband, Doug, (not his real name but a pseudonym to protect, the, uh, you know, the stupid), worked at a gas station in the neighborhood.

One day, Chuck the Pepsi driver needed to raise some money quickly to do some traveling. (my guess was to avoid alimony or some jail time) "He told my ex-husband that he was selling Pepsi for one dollar a Carton. Cheap huh? Good deal, huh? Only thing was, you had to buy all 800 cases that he had, AND the goddamn truck! THE WHOLE FUCKING TRUCK! My stupid husband thought that was a hell of a deal and gave him all our savings. Dumb son of a bitch up and left me right after that and so I have been left with this for the last 40 years. Me and the kids went through the Pepsi quick enough, but I got that stupid truck here, just waiting for the law to come after me for good reason."

Well, I'm no lawyer, but Pat actually is. She suggested that Delma talk to one, because it's almost positive that the statute of limitations had expired on that years ago.

I'll never look at a Pepsi or a goat in the same way again.

CHAPTER 19

Jesus Saves and Nobody Walks

*W*hen Pat and I were driving around aimlessly ringing doorbells and bothering waitresses, bartenders, and assorted musicians, we slowly developed some sixth sense of ferreting out a story. This is how we stumbled upon "Jesus Jerry" and his Church of "What's Happening Now."

Southern Illinois is a very pretty area with lots of straight flat highways, both State and Interstate. We like the state roads up in the Northern Area (Quad Cities Area) area and this particular story took us once again there. As we got a late start, we were still driving as 5PM came along. Pat started trying to tune the radio to WSIE, a local University of Southern Illinois station that plays a DJ that those of us who have an affinity for blues music just love. Papa Ray is a local STL area musician who found a home on the dial here every Monday evening. Lucky we found a hotel that was high enough in the few hills to be found up here. We got settled into our room and went into one of the bars that looked clean enough and dirty enough. I bought a round for the house and then asked the girl running the bar if we could listen to some "blues". She was young enough that she didn't know what I was talking about, although a few of the patrons said "hell yeah" to my request. I asked if I could change the radio to one of the WSIE affiliates that was sure to be playing "the blues". Well, we made a few friends that night and I am sure that we converted at least the barmaid to blues music!

This was a very close community who didn't particularly like outsiders and it was outside of this community where we got our actual story. On a beautiful spring day, we decided to start down the road once again. Sometimes the road just calls to you and you have to go.

Wanderlust has been in my veins for years yet I have no idea where it came from. My parents were the types who would just as soon stay at home than go on a vacation and explore, but not for lack of anything better to do. They were both children of the depression and had built a very nice home-life through academia and business involvements and investments. I think that the furthest they got from the USA was a trip to Puerto Rico and a trip or two to Canada.

Myself, on the other hand, I found a lot of fun and adventure when I had to go to another country that I might only not have heard of before, but certainly did not speak the language. So here in the safety of the USA, I didn't really have a language barrier, although I did learn to develop an ear of the local dialect and tried to mimic it as best that I could.

For example, if I were to find myself traveling through Bemidji Minnesota, I found it best if I *"Spoke a bit more like dem locals, don't cha' know? Eh?"* And when in the deep south, it is always polite to refer to *"The wah of Nawthen Aggression(?,"* rather than the Civil War.

Back to the story. Jesus Jerry and his church really didn't fit anywhere in my linguistic interests, but more for my curiosity of what sinister acts could be occurring behind these doors? Although we weren't really allowed in the actual barns where this was happening, the back story goes somewhat like this:

"Jesus Jerry" is a fire and brimstone type of Baptist preacher and his congregation likes it fine, just that way.

After many failed attempts to bring him out of the 1950's Baptist church teaching and into the present, he was cut off from the prescribed American Baptist Convention in King of Prussia Pennsylvania. This, when all be told, was just a minor inconvenience at best and did not stop *anything* from continuing the way "Jesus Jerry" liked it.

As a matter of fact, Jerry and the congregation found that they had MORE money at the end of each month, and, as they no longer were required to pay anything back to the Baptist Church administrative body, soon found themselves enjoying a much higher standard of living!

Every once in a while the Elders of the Church would come down and audit "Jesus Jerry" and the congregation. But try as they would, could never find any discrepancies. The books looked clean, the properties were kept up and, after decades of trying, they got tired of it and just decided to let him be. He's not bothering us, so we'll just ignore him, was their thought. Although a popular attraction to the locals, darned if the Elders could figure out why; they'd just as soon he'd go away.

Over the years, while all the other congregations were joining up with Habitat for Humanity, Unesco, The Baptists Children's Fund, as well as their own traveling ministries and missions to underserved countries, "The Church of What's Happening Now" found a nice little niche in their own backyard. They decided that the congregation was to provide reliable transportation by giving fully inspected, reliable, used cars to anyone who was in need. We are talking about reliable cars, nothing fancy and nothing expensive. "Jesus Jerry" once bragged that the average cost of one of his "giveaway cars" was no more than $35 each! The church was reaching out to many poor rural areas around northern Illinois, Wisconsin and Indiana. It seems that there is an undying need for reliable transportation within his congregation's reach. Their motto was,

"Jesus Saves, but nobody walks!"

And when you drove away in one of their cars, there was a bumper sticker on it saying just that.

All well and good, they worked very hard to stay under the radar of local media until one day the roof fell in. "Jesus Jerry" is now doing time, along with some of his other ministers in this church. It seems that "Jesus Jerry's" foot soldiers were just run of the mill, Chicago street punks, that would carjack cars from other punks and bad people (at least that was what they promised "Jesus Jerry"). They would have them sent to Jerry's farm where the parts would be stripped, serial numbers ground down and changed and then rebuilt into reliable transportation. The back room office of his church had the means to reproduce titles and registrations by making it appear these vehicles were from states with rather lenient registration and titling laws. Things move SO much faster when you don't have to deal with bureaucracy, paperwork and government, uh, how you say it in English; "crap?"

Since they were stealing older cars, no one really paid much attention, (word on the street was that the actual owners made out better with the insurance payment than they would have with an out and out trade in), and, the thieves had easy pickings. The thieves, mostly junkies and addicts, were happy for $20 to $35 to drive a car out to his place. Jerry's crew would rebuild the Toyotas and Nissans and turn them over to the congregation. This sounds very generous and benevolent, except Jerry, his "Ministers" and other employees of his church were taking some exorbitant tax write-offs. The added income more than allowed the group to pay a reasonable salary for each of "Jesus Jerry's" administrators or "gang", as well as give some pretty hefty bonuses and kickbacks to each other over the years. For each of the run of the mill Hondas, Nissans and Toyotas that they turned over, thousands of dollars would be made available for them to squander as they saw fit. Of all the other money that was brought in, washing it through rebuilding a regular "Hooptie" seemed to make sense and answer all the questions from the church auditors all the way up to and including the occasional nosey IRS auditors.

In their minds, that is the congregation's, it was all above board and legal. However, the FBI and IRS didn't see it that way. Every month or so, a BMW, Porsche or Audi was thrown into the mix, but "Jesus Jerry" and his crew got their choice of those when they came in. Oh, they paid a premium price for those cars. Sometimes up to 10 times the usual and customary prices for the beaters that were showing up.

$350 for a new Audi, Mercedes or Porsche? Good pickings if it comes your way alright. It was a wonder that these clowns didn't get tossed sooner as some of these guys were turning cars over once a month or less. Each one was making a nice side profit scamming these cars off on an unsuspecting public or congregant who sought trust and solace in this somehow religion of the car lots.

Some of the witnesses also speculated that the "Church" was even placing orders for these high end cars when they were feeling especially good about themselves. Crooks being crooks (similar to politicians) they always get greedier and greedier as well as bolder and bolder and I would add stupider and stupider.

All in all, it was a pretty lucrative business until the end. The auditors finally found that the amount of tax breaks and write-offs that they were claiming versus the actual cars values just didn't add up. The "Mother Church" was happy to turn their back once again on "Jesus Jerry" and his congregation when the Feds came by to investigate. They hung him out to dry.

Since some of these cars were heading out to Wisconsin and Indiana, the IRS was happy to turn over to the FBI, the contacts there and up in Chicago. It was a pretty messy deal even if the head church was not involved. There were a few of the congregation who were just innocent bystanders and watched their church, their beliefs and their lives just slide down the same slope "Jesus Jerry" and his minions went down.

When it was all over, "Jesus" Jerry McCain was doing time in a federal penitentiary in West Virginia. The last I heard, he would be ready for parole sometime in 2029, not a particularly long time as sentences go for usurping the trust of an entire congregation, but it should serve as punishment for his crimes and a deterrent to others of his minions who still may think this was a good idea.

You wonder why there has to be a separation of church and state; Just imagine if our politicians were involved.........

And no, "Jesus Jerry", DIDN'T walk.

CHAPTER 20

Nah, Those Computers Are Just A Passing Fad

*T*his one started out a bit different. I got a tip last week that I might find something up in Coal City. In my other life, I had been doing some research into coal mining including strip mining and long wall mining. Just a passing interest of mine as I drive though the pock marked state of Illinois. In my travels for the scientific and medical as well as my own companies over 50 years, I have been through a lot of Illinois and personally saw the scars left from turn of the century mining techniques. These did not have the health of the land nor the preservation of the land for future generations anywhere near the top of their list of priorities. As a matter of fact, Pat and I just got back from a trip to the Pinckneyville/DuQuoin area.

I drove that area extensively in the '70's and '80's. I saw the strip mining taking place and I saw the remains of what was left of the land. On one particular road, that I cannot remember for the life of me, I remember seeing a very old yet very LARGE coal shovel that was finished with its plunder and just left to rust. Now this thing had sat amongst the spoils piles for decades because it was just plain *old* even when I saw it. Rust had replaced any protective paint that was on it. I don't remember if I could see the bucket, but all the others of that size and age that I have seen since then would be able to scoop up a large truck with ease.

I woke up one morning last week and announced that we were off to find this shovel. I had spent the night before looking on Google Earth, and was able to focus in on the scars from its aerial views, however I was not able to locate any remaining shovel in that area. Of course the obvious thing to do was take a road trip. Pat agreed, (we've been married for 44 years now and I think she hangs around just to see what I'll do next. At least that's what my friends tell me.) Well that trip was a bust. We drove up and down, forth and back over roads that I remember and those that I didn't remember. Pat however, was new to this special scenery that we were seeing and didn't realize the scope of its damage until seeing it with her own eyes.

We have kept in touch with some of the people who have been subjects of these stories and some who didn't really make it into the wonderment of Barn Secrets. One such person sent me an e-mail and suggested that I might find an interesting item in a barn near Coal City, Illinois. I knew exactly where that was; just outside of Joliet. I have driven past it many times on my way to or from Chicago up Route 66 and its newer replacement, I-55. I had never stopped in there, but it was about 3 and a half hours from home straight up I-55. I remember the mountainous piles of earth that were displaced to make way for the mining equipment; piles of overburden that these massive steam-driven and later, electric-driven shovels moved out of the way while following the coal seam.

In the old days they just left the piles. In time the rain would wash all sorts of turned up minerals into the pits around them. The piles themselves also would try and reclaim the land by growing weeds, trees, scrub and anything else that tried to adhere to its steep surfaces.

We were just about 3 and a half hours out when the GPS told us to exit I-55 as we were near our destination. Another twenty minutes and we pulled into the driveway. I had called in advance and set up a meeting. When I described our project over the phone, Mr. Fenaka was happy enough to have us come up and see his modern marvel of the computer age, a circa 1950 Sperry Rand Univac One that is taking up space in his barn.

Barry Fenaka met us as we stepped out of the car and stretched from the long ride. It was an early February afternoon and we were given the lay of the land, so to speak. Barry had bought this farm from the bank a couple of years ago in hopes of selling it to the neighbor on the farm next to it. Barry was an accountant with a group of investors from Sacramento who thought that Illinois was due for a land boom. It is almost all flat through the center and the farms were consolidating and otherwise, just selling off for pennies on the dollar.

After their purchase, they found that the information they were given and relied upon was worthless. Not as worthless as the land, but close. This place was owned by the Walters family before and that is who they had inherited this Electronic Brain from. There was a lot of equipment under the old tarps that must have been there for decades. It was obvious to see that the farm varmints and critters had chewed through wires, Bakelite knobs, corners and switches. A few chairs had most of the stuffing pulled out of them, most every glass panel was missing or broken. There were crates of wires and cables and switch panels. There were at least 2 operating consoles that I could see and one looked like someone had taken an axe to it. Many cables that were sticking out of other electronic cabinets were also cut in such a way that it looked like someone just wanted to get it out of wherever it was FAST.

Barry was trying to sell me on this farm. We again explained the book and that was the only reason that we were here, so he backed off for a while. He did have a back story on the computer though.

Web Walters had purchased this farm in the early 1930's when he returned from a trip to Europe with his new British Bride, Betty. His parents, who were quite well off, had given him a start in life with a college savings fund. Web took a trip and educated himself instead. When they returned, he used what money was left to put a down payment on the farm and they started to raise their family. Their only son Scott was born in 1934 and was a "whiz kid" in math as Barry told it. He went to the Coal City schools, skipped a bunch of grades and when time came to graduate high school at 12 years old, Web and Betty used their connections in England to get Scott a scholarship to Cambridge University. They didn't feel right sending him away at such a young age, so he stayed around the farm and spent a few years over the next 6 years off and on at a relative's house in Chicago attending Northwestern. He finished his Bachelor of Science by the time he was 19 and was sent to Cambridge to acquire a diploma in Numerical Analysis and Automated Computing, a very new field that Scott excelled in. He was asked to stay on and teach for a few years and then in the 1950's came back to the US and landed a very prestigious job at Sperry Rand working on....you guessed it, the Univac One program. The fledgling computer field was just perfect for him and he traveled all over the world demonstrating the workings of this new device. When he wasn't traveling with the "Brain", he was at home developing programs to make it work faster and more efficiently, a talent that fit him like a glove.

Being from Coal City, Scott had an affinity for this area and also a need to come back and see if he could use some of his talents and the "computer age" to help this depressed area of the state. Chicago seemed to have it all, but anything south of the loop soon trailed off to desolate farms and farms waiting to be made more desolate by the coal mining industry.

On one of his trips to demonstrate the computer, he wound up at the University of Illinois at Champaign/Urbana, one of the older universities in the state. He was presenting a seminar which was attended by quite a few scientists and geologists from the coal companies around the area.

Scott was soon spending more and more time with these people and fit right in with them. They were working with the computer to maximize yield in strip mining and developing a newer use of an older method called long wall mining. Scott and his friends at the coal companies soon realized that the data was already out there regarding long-wall and strip mining. All of the companies had it and didn't realize the treasure that they held. Although none of the companies wanted to invest in the quickly escalating price of this computer, they all were soon convinced of the need. Scott developed a consortium of scientists, geologists, coal field specialists…...you know, Brains in a chair. Sperry was tired of letting Scott's pet project take precedence over the real sales to be made with many agencies of the US government, General Motors, US Steel and the like. These little pet projects were a drain in their profits..

Then something turned. Scott quit Sperry Rand while keeping his scientific group active. He found that he could entice investors to help keep his group alive and also help fund his project. A plan was developing in his mind also. He would rent out the basement of the local VFW Hall, where his father was a member in pretty high standing.

His group would continue working there on the program development while Scott would gather investors to assist in buying their OWN computer. Well, not so much their OWN, *per se*. Sperry would sell a license to use their computer as long as you used their software. For all intents and purposes, it was thought of as ownership, however, the Univac would always remain property of the Sperry Company. Now this was a multi-year project and sometime in 1956, Sperry introduced the new Univac II which was much more powerful than the original. Scott's new plan was to acquire one of the old scrap model I Univac for pennies on the dollar. According to him, it would do the same thing that they needed, just not anywhere as fast as the new one. This plan was left out of the information when speaking to the other participants. When they had the final check to purchase the supposed new computer for somewhere north of half a million dollars, Scott, instead, switched the deal and picked up the trade-in for about $1,200 (estimated scrap value). And of course he financed the balance, another part of his plan that his group was in the dark about. Everything appeared to be on the up and up, although if you looked closely at the paperwork, it was obvious you bought an older piece of scrap rather than the license for the newest unit. According to Barry, no one picked up on the difference or if they did, they were not questioning it.

The geeks had their toy and were happily churning out data bits, the investors were happy to see the data coming out although none had any idea what the data actually was, and Scott was soon happy enough spending time in Las Vegas with some new friends and lots of money. Scott was very at ease with these new friends, which may have even included some of the Rat Pack as introduced to him by a poolside acquaintance, Miss Dorothy Smith, a midwestern beauty who liked to flee the St. Louis winters for the sun and fun of Las Vegas. Apparently these two spent some time together and even planned a few rendezvous when they would each have a break in their schedule and could coordinate it. Somehow Scott still had access to Sperry's private plane and when he didn't, he wasn't shy about asking the guys in Sperry's avionics department if he could get a ride to Vegas on one of the many planes Sperry Avionics had in the air any given day. He would just have to drive to Rock Island, Midway, or Meigs Field to catch the flight. A good thing this was not taking place a few years later. The Honorable Mayor Richard Daily decided one day that he didn't like that FAA Registered Airport on "his" Lake Front and using the darkness of one night, had his street department dig very large "X"'s up and down its main runway stranding more that one plane there on the ground and making at least one pilot ask for a substitute runway, because "Miegs" was "GONE!!?!"?"

And People wonder why we "downstaters"sometimes want to "secede" from Chicago.

Meanwhile:

Every once in a while, a question would come up about the 'new' computer that Sperry had, but Scott had the gift and was always able to convince anyone that this was indeed a transition computer that may have looked like the older version, but had all the upgrades of the newest one. When the geeks got to questioning their now slower computer, Scott would come in late at night and "clean up" his colleagues' programming to make it run faster and more efficiently (his specialty). Then, after collecting a few more investors, he would magically unleash his new programs on the old equipment but first telling everyone that Sperry had just upgraded the hardware to the most recent version. Everyone was amazed at the improvement from the new equipment. It was amazing how a couple of crates marked "Sperry" that were full of junk could make such an improvement on performance. Scott thought "Life is good when you're on the con!"

By this time Scott was collecting more money than he knew what to do with, but he found a way. Wine, women and song, the rest he just pissed away as was described by one witness at the trial. Yes, it had come to that. Scott was spending less time with his geeks and more time with his Vegas friends so that when the geeks had a problem with the computer one day, instead of calling Scott, they called Sperry.

Then it all came out. Sperry had no idea what computer they were using. There was no record of Scott's group ever qualifying for a Univac I License *much* less a Univac II. The house of cards quickly began to fall. Sperry sent some techs out to the VFW Hall basement, and were shocked to see an old Univac Model I running some very sophisticated programs, but nothing that they had on their books.

The lawyers got involved, the police, the scientific community and even the family. Sperry employees came in to repossess the computer and were met with a certain reluctance by the geeks to let them take it. They came back the next day with twice the number of techs and one big guy swinging a fire axe at every cable coming from the back of each machine. That was it. The computer was done.

All of this happened over the course of about 2 weeks. Certainly not enough time to gather up the computer and get it out of there, but there was enough time for Scott to clean out every bank account associated with this endeavor and disappear.

The investors got nothing as, by the time the computer was being reclaimed, the Sperry accounting department declared that the value of that computer was nil and that it would cost more to ship it back than it was worth. The engineers that inspected it found that everything would have been in better shape if the big guy with the fire axe had turned *off* the electricity BEFORE he started swinging the axe and chopping cables. It made for a very dramatic repo show though, lots of yelling, chopping, and sparks, well it must have looked a lot like the fireworks at the fourth of July picnic that the VFW sponsored every year down by the lake.

Web was asked to take that piece of junk out of the basement of the VFW and was stripped of his honorable standing in the organization. He managed to get the Univac I back to his barn where it sits to this day.

The scientists all went back to be absorbed into academia and the geologists and coal field specialists were assumed to be absorbed back into the land.

During the trial, which made a lot of noise, spent a lot of money and pointed a lot of fingers, only one participant was missing; Scott Walters. Web and Betty were there each day watching and listening to the story of their rogue son whom they now missed very much. Hoping to find someone who knew of his whereabouts, they suffered through the insults and innuendos each day as it went on.

The trial went on for about 2 months and the prosecutor brought in every kind of witness he could think of, but in the end, no one knew where Scott might be. One witness said that he met him up in Iowa where he mentioned something about developing a new way to reclaim land using water and some form of newly reshaped CO_2 molecules using ultrasound. He was driving a Red MGA convertible sports car. He also said he needed someone to print up a medical degree and physics doctorate from MIT………..

CHAPTER 21

Bulgarian Wedding Music, Now Why Didn't I Think Of That?

*M*any times Pat and I had driven on Old State Route 1 running north and south in Illinois from Chicago to Cave-in-Rock on the Ohio River. This is one of the oldest standing routes in the state. This is one of the first roads, or more likely, paths. I can always imagine settlers walking this path or maybe on horseback. With enough traffic, it eventually became one of the first state roads, was paved and given the designation as State Route 1. A pretty good bit of history is packed in between these shoulders. This little area I have passed through delivering boats, yachts and other vessels as a side gig. I earned a 100 Master Mariners Certificate from the United Stated Merchant Marine Corps back in the mid 2000's. Hell, they practically give one to anybody who can prove physical and mental capabilities along with showing proof of 720 days standing watch on the particular class vessel you are working with. I earned mine with my own vessel and others the I delivered over the years running up and down the Mississippi, Missouri, Illinois, Ohio and lots of others over the past 30 years. Oh yeah, the Great Lakes and Gulf of Mexico were also included destinations. Cave in Rock on the Ohio River just above Golconda always beckoned me as I passed by it through the years traveling up or down the Ohio River. This time, however, I was driving the Sequoia through Elizebethstown when I told Pat we were going to take a short detour. You see Cave in Rock is a unique geological formation of a cave, washed out of the rocks on the western descending bank of the Ohio river. I first heard of it when *How The West Was Won* was released in the early 1960's in Transfix Cinema Theatre which were a combination of three projector systems plus lots more technology that I am leaving out for brevity here. Please research this some more as it does need to be resurrected in my humble opinion. Cave in Rock was featured in that film as a hide-out for River Pirates. Jimmy Stewart, one of many stars of that film, was left for dead by a pirate group. Pat and I walked the small path the lead to the cave and were able to walk through it and make photographs of this phenomenal feature. Make a day trip there sometime, it is well worth your time!

Well, here it is a very cold Monday in March, Casimir Pulaski Day in Illinois, A Polish Nobleman who was also known as the Father of the American Cavalry after being recommended by Benjamin Franklin to assist in the American Revolutionary War. A little known holiday in all parts of the world except for Poland of course, and Illinois of all things. Well, it turns out that Chicago at some point had more Polish citizens than Warsaw Poland, and being the politically friendly thing to do, they made it a state holiday. Gotta get those votes wherever you can. And before anyone jumps the gun, although I was not born in Illinois, my grandmother on my mothers side was a Kobalevski from Poland.

We had never heard the story of the pirate radio station on Route 1 though. In doing some research, we learned that almost as soon as commercial radio had established itself in automobiles, there was always some sort of pirate radio station operating up and down this road. It was not commercial. It was not on at a regular time. It was, however, against all the rules and regulations of the FCC, both at the time of start-up and as the industry grew. No one could ever tell you where it was operating from, or who would be running it. From our scant research, there are many low-power pirate radio stations around the world, the USA and most specifically, Illinois. Even today. You just have to be interested enough to look. In the days when radio was new, and the receivers were very large, not everyone had the luxury to afford one. And even if you did, you still needed to be close enough to pick up their low power signal. Kids and enthusiasts built crystal sets and would always be fascinated with whatever they picked up. As the radio industry grew, the government found that there were jobs to be had and money to be made regulating it. In regulating it, the government recognized this to be a very important "utility" for mass communication. A sort of one way event. And this fit the government like a glove. They could broadcast a message to many thousands of people at once, with the added benefit of not having to listen to the feedback, opinions or complaints of any of those thousands who tuned it. When the FCC was established it was to keep it clear, clean and free for just this purpose.

This is where the Pirate radio stations grew their niche. For every commercial radio station, (think radio commercials and how much money they brought in along with licensing fees to the government as long as they could control this) there were pirate stations popping up to broadcast information that wasn't necessarily fitting for the commercial stations who lost ad revenue, the people who tuned in to it (according to the regulators), nor the government who lost out on licensing fees and taxes. This was a pirate industry at best and the government is in its right to go after them and shut them down. Which they did. I won't argue that there was a lot of censorship involved back then, but the radio industry was in its infancy and was just feeling growing pains. With the advent of the digital age, car radio and now most home radio stations are pre-tuned and locked into the main frequency. The days of tuning your radio tuner a little to the left or a little to the right until you have the signal you are looking for are all but forgotten. Your radios will lock onto the strongest signal, even if you are looking for the lesser powered station right next to it. With today's equipment, it assumes that you will want the strongest signal and will give it to you, want it or not.

Nowadays, you may find a pirate station if you look for one, but you won't be surprised at it's content. No, these days it's pretty benign. No freedom fighters or revolutionaries, at least not here in the USA, which brings us back to this story.

We were traveling along the road and noticed a farm house with a very nice set of antennae around the house. We could see them from the road. From my days as a radio engineer, I had a First Class Commercial License when I graduated from tech school, I could tell that this was a fairly sophisticated amateur radio set up. A lot of people have become amateur or "Ham" radio operators with just a simple interest in radio, electronics, communications, or just technology in general. There are also some who decided to get into the hobby after retiring from the radio and television industry, sort of a "busman's holiday" if you will......

We walked up to the front door of the house, not a turn of the century Victorian style with clapboard siding, no, this one was just a brick ranch style which may date from the 1960's. Nothing special about the architecture, no, it was still the number and size of the antennae as well as the wires and cables that crisscrossed the yard strung between the towers, the house and the barn that got my curiosity stirred up. All in all, it looked like a very substantial installation.

The door was opened and I half expected a "Doc Brown" character from one of the "Back to the Future" franchises. The gentleman who opened the door was cordial as I began my spiel. I had become quite good at explaining our project with just enough zeal to hook them with interest, and enough sincerity to get them sympathetic enough to ask more about it. (If you can fake sincerity, you've got it made.)

When I inserted that extra part about having a 1st class ticket from back in the 70's, I had him. He introduced himself as Frank Bermann, a retired radio engineer from the Chicago area. He and his wife wanted to stay close to the area where his grown children were raising their grandkids up in the Chicago suburbs. Frank and his wife Katie felt that a nice farm would be a change from the city life of Chicago.

About that time, one of the rootinest, tootinest hombres on this side of the Pecos came running through the house with cap guns ablazin'! Frank was still talking to us and looking us straight in the eye when, without missing a beat, he reached his arm out and corralled this miniature whirling dervish before any harm was done to Pat or me.

"This is one of them," Frank said as he hoisted the kid, still squirming, up to ride his back. "Liam here spends the weekends with us as much as we want. Never expected to have so much fun with a 6 year old. It's just hard to keep up with him." I told him ours was the same way and then asked "Did they vaccinate yours with a phonograph needle?" "Oh, yeah, he's just a fountain of questions."

We were invited in and met his wife Katie who looked like she had just escaped from the *Ransom of Red Chief*…..and was happy to be out! "Nice meeting you," she said, as she walked past us, out the door and took off down the gravel driveway spewing rocks everywhere in her wake. Frank put Liam down and said, "She was planning on shopping today, so it looks like it's just us and the kid."

We spent the afternoon with Frank and Liam listening to his stories of Chicago radio, the rock and roll revolution and the heydays of radio. He did let us in on a little secret that he felt safe in telling us and letting us share.

Frank had been an FCC Liaison in Chicago and worked as a volunteer arbitrator between the FCC and commercial stations in the region. It seems he gathered enough information about pirate radio stations that he decided to "dabble" in the field when he retired. He showed me his phased array antenna system that he designed and his mobile transmitter in his car that acted as a roving antenna.

Without getting too technical, this was a small way that he discovered how to elude the FCC when they are trying to track down a radio station with their range and directional finders. You see, any transmitter when operating, sends out a signal that is just too easy to "home" in on, something no pirate wants. Frank's design of his antenna system was a series of antennae that sent signals out in such a way that it would appear to be transmitting from someplace where it wasn't. Aided by his small transmitter in his car and his Radio Shack TRS 80 computer (his first) plus a few pretty powerful Dell laptops, he was able to bounce his signal to make it appear that it was transmitting from anywhere but from where he was.

When he first started this hobby, he was sort of politically active and might have gotten the attention of the FCC until he figured out a nice little loophole in the "unwritten" rules and regs. If you broadcasted something that no one cared about, it gathered very little interest in the enforcement community. And so it was that on that day, Frank Bermann became the proud owner of a pirate radio station playing some Hawaiian and mostly Bulgarian Wedding music.

After a tour of his "station" and listening to more Bulgarian Wedding music than anyone other than a Bulgarian bride should have to, we bid goodbye to Frank and Liam.

With Cap guns a"blazin" as our final salute, we headed off into the sunset spewing rocks in every direction with the same need to "get the hell out of Dodge" as Katie had when she took off.

As we swung onto the state road, Pat turned on the radio. *The Road Goes on Forever and the Party Never Ends,* was just starting.